Modular Knits

Modular Knits

Iris Schreier's Innovative & Easy Techniques

Iris Schreier

LARK
CRAFTS

An Imprint of Sterling Publishing Co., Inc.
New York

WWW.LARKCRAFTS.COM

Editor: **Donna Druchunas**

Art Director: **Dana Irwin**

Photographer: **John Widman**

Cover Designer: **Megan Kirby**

Assistant Art Director: **Lance Wille**

Assistant Editor: **Rebecca Guthrie**

Associate Art Director: **Shannon Yokeley**

Illustrator: **Orrin Lundgren**

Editorial Assistance: **Delores Gosnell**

Editorial Intern: **Metta L. Pry**

The Library of Congress has cataloged the hardcover edition as follows:

Schreier, Iris.
    Modular knits: new techniques for today's knitters / Iris Schreier.
       p. cm.
    Includes index.
    ISBN 1-57990-649-4 (hardcover)
1. Knitting. I. Title.
TT820.S295 2005
746.43'2--dc22

10 9 8 7 6 5 4 3 2 1

Published by Lark Crafts
An Imprint of Sterling Publishing Co., Inc.
387 Park Avenue South, New York, NY 10016

First Paperback Edition 2011
Text © 2005, Iris Schreier
Photography and illustrations © 2005, Lark Crafts, an Imprint of Sterling
Publishing Co., Inc.

Distributed in Canada by Sterling Publishing,
c/o Canadian Manda Group, 165 Dufferin Street
Toronto, Ontario, Canada M6K 3H6

Distributed in the United Kingdom by GMC Distribution Services,
Castle Place, 166 High Street, Lewes, East Sussex, England BN7 1XU

Distributed in Australia by Capricorn Link (Australia) Pty Ltd.
P.O. Box 704, Windsor, NSW 2756 Australia

If you have questions or comments about this book, please contact:
Lark Crafts
67 Broadway
Asheville, NC 28801
828-253-0467

Manufactured in China

ISBN 13: 978-1-57990-649-8 (hardcover) 978-1-60059-797-8 (paperback)

For information about custom editions, special sales, premium and corporate purchases, please contact Sterling Special Sales Department at 800-805-5489 or specialsales@sterlingpub.com.

For information about desk and examination copies available to college and university professors, requests must be submitted to academic@larkbooks.com. Our complete policy can be found at www.larkcrafts.com.

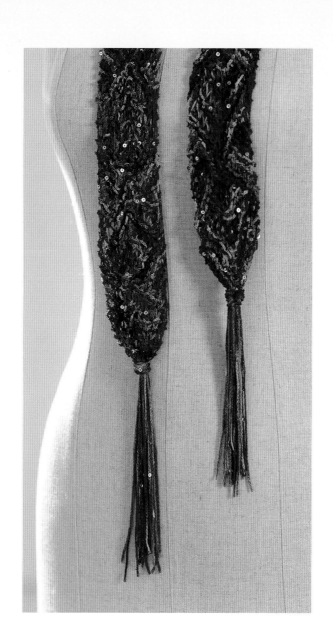

CONTENTS

Introduction. 8

CHAPTER 1: BASICS OF MODULAR KNITTING
WITH SHORT ROWS. 11

CHAPTER 2: VERTICAL AND HORIZONTAL
GARTER STITCH SQUARES 19

Patchwork Eyeglass Case 22

Basketweave Pillow 24

CHAPTER 3: DIAGONAL TRIANGLES
AND DIAMONDS. 26

Multi-Directional Scarf 31

Starburst Shawl 34

Felted Geometric Tote 38

Flat-Top Hat 42

Zigzag Scarf 45

CHAPTER 4: UNMITERED OR
CENTER-INCREASE SHAPES. 48

Elegant Table Runner 52

Lace Ribbon Poncho 56

Building Blocks Shawl 60

Chevron Tie 63

CHAPTER 5: OTHER SHORT ROW SHAPES 66

Holes Scarf 70

Bull's-Eye Hat 72

Square Holes Sweater 76

CHAPTER 6: CENTER-DECREASE
KNITTING SHAPES 80

Pinwheel Purse 84

Zebra Afghan 88

Hidden Square Pillow 93

CHAPTER 7: WORKING WITH
MULTIPLE SHAPES. 96

Diamond Blossom Scarf 98

Sequined Evening Sash 101

Sheer One-Piece Shawl 104

Diamond Panel Vest 109

Elegant Openwork Poncho 114

Cozy Diamond Wrap 118

Mirrored Angles Scarf 122

ACKNOWLEDGMENTS 126

ABOUT THE AUTHOR 127

INDEX. 128

INTRODUCTION

A re you interested in achieving the modular effect without following elaborate charts and graphs, and without picking up stitches and cutting yarn every time you create a shape? Well, you are in luck! Here's an innovative method for creating triangles, diamonds, and squares that's very easy and removes many of the obstacles in learning to knit modularly. I invented it by accident while knitting on the diagonal with variegated yarns. The Multi-Directional Scarf on page 31, my first design and the one that originated the concept of continuous modular knitting, generated so much attention that I realized I was on to something special. All it requires is simple garter stitch and easy short-row techniques. The other techniques presented in this book are easy to learn, too. The only danger is that once you become comfortable using these techniques, you probably won't be able to stop!

We are accustomed to straight lines in knitwear. Modules present the unexpected—strange crossings and intersections, vertical and horizontal lines right next to one another, even symmetrical bull's eyes—and the results can be spectacular. Modular knitting is not a new idea; various techniques called piecework knitting or patchwork knitting have been around for decades. Some say Virginia Woods Bellamy invented modular knitting in her book Number Knitting, written in the 1940s. In the 1990s, Horst Schultz created many new modular shapes based on those original techniques. His patchwork knitting books are breathtakingly beautiful. One of the most concise yet informative books on mitered shapes is Vivian Hoxbro's Domino Knitting. All of these incredibly talented designers followed the premise that modular knitting is made up of individual pieces. The modules are knitted, bound off, the yarn is usually cut, stitches are picked up, and new modules are knitted onto the old modules to expand the garment. My continuous knitting technique simplifies the process and eliminates cutting yarn and picking up stitches. Each shape looks like a separate section in your garment, but it is actually connected to other shapes, and all the stitches remain live on the needles at all times.

The first four chapters of this book describe various shapes and designs that can be made continuously. The fifth covers traditional piecework knitting for comparison. I have included step-by-step instructions to help you learn to knit each shape before you begin a project. Each practice session can be completed in less than an hour, and after you have completed the small swatch, you will have the confidence and skill to knit the related projects.

I originally developed the techniques in this book to enhance the appearance of variegated yarn. Like many knitters out there, I adore working with this type of yarn, particularly the hand-painted varieties—it is so much fun never knowing how the colors will come out. The surprise reduces some of the monotony of knitting and keeps me going. However, I have been disappointed with variegated yarn when it knits up in unattractive patches, which is often the case in traditionally knitted items. This problem is eliminated in multi-directional knitting. The Basketweave Pillow on page 24 stripes the variegated yarn in small squares and the Zigzag Scarf on page 45 creates diagonal intersections of stripes.

As I continued to experiment with knitting squares, triangles, and diamonds, I found that they also work well with solid yarns, particularly in two-color combinations. The Bull's-Eye Hat on page 72 shows how easy it is to combine two solid colors into a fantastic design that looks complicated but is actually quite simple.

One of the most important advantages of modular knitting, whether continuously or in piecework, is that it helps garments keep their shape over time. Garter stitch tends to "grow," or lose its shape, by becoming longer and narrower due to gravity and the weight of the garment. The multidirectional modules are always pulling the garment in various directions, preventing sagging and loss of shape.

Please keep in mind that the continuous techniques presented here have not eliminated the need for piecework knitting, but they have added more options for the knitter interested in achieving the modular effect in a less complicated fashion.

I hope you will work up practice swatches of each shape. As you learn new skills, you will also have fun and create beautiful and unique garments that can enhance your love of knitting.

Basics of Modular Knitting with Short Rows

BASICS OF MODULAR KNITTING WITH SHORT ROWS

If you have basic knitting skills and you know how to cast on, bind off, knit, increase, and decrease, you can make the projects in this book. Spend some time knitting the practice swatches at the beginning of each chapter, and you'll find that the patterns become much easier to follow.

Gauge is not very straightforward in most of these patterns because they are multidirectional. In order to help you with your yarn selection, I've listed the weight of the yarn I used along with the gauge provided on the ball band. Where it was not possible to measure gauge conventionally on the knitted garment, I've listed the gauge for a particular module, so that you can knit a sample swatch and compare the measurements.

Because of all the turning used in this approach to modular knitting, it is likely that your stitch count may occasionally be off by just a few stitches. If your project looks good visually, just keep going and add extra stitches or remove some to get back to the required number of stitches. The beauty in this system is its flexibility, so enjoy the knitting. Note that in most of these patterns the shape of the knitting will not immediately be apparent. So knit a minimum of 5" (12.7cm) at which time you can see the shape emerge.

EXPERIENCE LEVELS

There are four experience levels used in this book: Beginner, Easy, Intermediate, and Advanced. A Beginner level is an ideal first modular knitting project—even if you are a new knitter who has never knit anything other than a scarf. I suggest that you knit the practice swatches at the beginning of each chapter and make several Beginner and Easy projects before you move on to the Intermediate and Advanced projects. This will help you get the hang of the system, while at the same time boosting your confidence.

The projects are ranked relative to one another, so do not be put off by the Intermediate or Advanced ratings. Once you are comfortable with the techniques used in modular knitting, you will be ready for any of the Advanced projects. The chart on page 12 will help you select projects for your skill level.

■ BEGINNER

These projects are appropriate for knitters who have never worked on modular knitting projects before. They use only one modular shape and are small projects that can be completed in a weekend. Be sure to work through the practice swatch before starting a project. The Basketweave Pillow on page 24 is a perfect first project.

■■ EASY

After you have learned to knit the shapes and made a beginner project, you will be ready to try the easy projects. These use only one modular shape, but they may include multiple yarns or unusual shaping. If the project includes a shape you have not made before, make sure to knit the practice swatch at the beginning of the chapter before you begin.

■■■ INTERMEDIATE

These projects are for those knitters ready to go beyond the basics of modular knitting. Some have openwork panels, some use multiple modular shapes, and others have more complex shaping or color changes. They are not difficult, but they require more concentration than the easier projects.

■■■■ ADVANCED

If you are an expert knitter or if you have already made several of the projects from this book, the advanced projects will stretch your skills and provide an exciting challenge. These projects all include multiple modular shapes.

YARN AND NEEDLES

Hand-painted and variegated yarns show off the shapes of continuously knitted projects with beautiful results. Combining two solid yarns, alternating them for maximum effect, also creates striking designs. You can watch patterns in color develop as you turn and knit with the yarn in small sections, as opposed to the usual way of knitting straight across. Stripes form, and these are particularly interesting on the diagonal. The shapes make your knitting more interesting, and best of all, although they look impressive, they are quite easy to make.

Pick needles that are as short as you can work with, considering the number of stitches called for by the project. I prefer using 7"/17.8cm needles; however, these are difficult to come by. I often use double-pointed needles in my projects because they are more widely available in shorter lengths. Putting a point protector on one end of a double-pointed needle turns it into a short single-pointed needle. Because you turn frequently as you knit the shapes, shorter needles are more comfortable and easier to handle.

In addition, select the smoothest needles that you can afford. The most comfortable needles I've worked with are rosewood needles like the ones shown on the left. They are soft on the hands and polished so beautifully that the yarn doesn't catch on them.

KNITTING ABBREVIATIONS

BO Bind off.

Use any technique you are comfortable with. (For tips on binding off loosely, see page 16.)

CO Cast on.

In most cases you may use any technique you are comfortable with. When a special cast-on technique is required, this is specified in the pattern. (For instructions on casting on loosely, see page 14.)

dyo Drop yarn over.

This technique is used to make elongated stitches. When instructed in a pattern, drop the yarn overs created on the previous row. The next stitch will stretch into an elongated stitch. When this is done over an entire row, it creates a lovely openwork panel.

k1inc1 Knit one, increase one.

Knit 1 stitch through the front of a stitch, and leaving the stitch on the needle, knit a second stitch through the back of the same stitch, creating 2 stitches out of 1 stitch (increase).

k1tblinc1 Knit one through back loop, increase one through front loop.

Knit 1 stitch through back loop of a stitch, and leaving the stitch on the needle, knit a second stitch through the front of the same stitch, creating 2 stitches out of 1 stitch (increase).

m1k1 Make 1, knit 1.

Make 1 stitch by picking up a loop through the bar between the stitch just knitted and the next stitch on the left needle. Put the new loop on the left needle. Then knit both the loop and the next stitch on the left needle together, removing both stitches from the left needle and putting the new stitch on the right needle.

pm Place marker.

In Center-Increase Diamonds you will use 3 markers per row, one to mark the middle increases, and two on either side to mark the end of each row to be attached to surrounding shapes. This is explained in detail on page 51.

psso Pass slipped stitch over.

Always comes after a slipped stitch followed by a knit or k2tog. Pass the previously slipped stitch over the stitch just knitted. This removes 1 stitch (decrease).

rm Remove marker.

Remove the stitch marker as indicated in the pattern. You may be instructed to place the marker at a different place in the work on the next row.

s1 Slip 1.

Slip 1 stitch knitwise from the left needle to the right needle with the yarn held in back.

s1, k2tog, psso Slip 1, knit 2 together, pass slipped stitch over.

Slip 1 stitch knitwise from the left needle to the right needle with the yarn held in back. Knit the next 2 stitches together. Then, pass previously slipped stitch over the new stitch just knitted. This creates 1 stitch out of 3 stitches (double decrease).

s1wyif Slip 1 with yarn in front.

Slip 1 stitch purlwise from the left needle to the right needle with the yarn held in front.

s2psso Slip 2 stitches, and pass first slipped stitch over second slipped stitch.

Slip 1 stitch knitwise, slip a second stitch knitwise, pass the first slipped stitch over the second slipped stitch (decrease).

skp Slip 1, knit 1, pass slipped stitch over.

Slip 1 stitch knitwise through back loop, knit the next stitch, pass the slipped stitch over the knit stitch, and drop it off the needle as when binding off. This creates 1 stitch out of 2 stitches (decrease).

turn Turn.

Turn work around and begin knitting in the other direction even if you have not completed a row. This is the key to continuous modular knitting. Watch the instructions carefully when you are learning to knit a new modular shape. Sometimes you will see a line that says *do not turn*.

yo Yarn over.

Bring the yarn between the needles to the front, and then over the needle again to the back of the work to begin the next knit stitch.

To work a double yarn over, bring the yarn between the needles to the front, and then over the needle again to the back of the work, then repeat. You should have two wraps of yarn around the right needle before you make the next knit stitch.

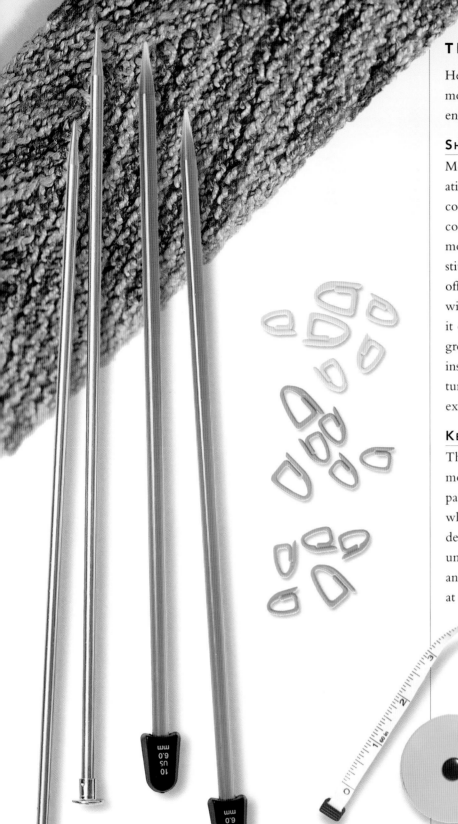

TECHNIQUES

Here are some specific techniques that I use in modular knitting. Using these techniques will ensure that you succeed with these projects.

SHORT ROWS

Modular knitting has traditionally been about creating modules that are decreased in size in their construction down to a single stitch. However, the concept of the continuous method is to grow the modules. As the modules grow, more and more stitches will be on your needles. Instead of binding off the module when it is at its desired size, you will be instructed to add another shape to balance it out and maintain a flat fabric. In addition to growing modules, you will find the patterns instructing you to turn your work midstream. The turns are called "short rows," and they are used extensively throughout these projects.

KEEPING TRACK OF WHERE YOU ARE

There is a system to the process of continuous modular knitting that I've developed. Most of the patterns use stitch markers to help you determine where to do the next k1inc1 increase or skp decrease. In fact, there are visual cues that you'll uncover that help you get rid of the stitch markers and understand where you are and what is required at all times. The k1inc1 is always knitted into the last stitch of the previous row's k1inc1, a visually shorter stitch that is identifiable.

The skp is used to close the gap between the previous row's slipped stitch and the new, yet unknitted, stitches from the shape you are joining.

LOOSE CAST ON

In modular knitting, it is important to cast on loosely, particularly when knitting on the diagonal (see page 28). I found a very

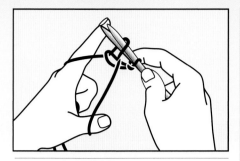

Figure 1

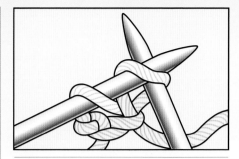

Figure 2

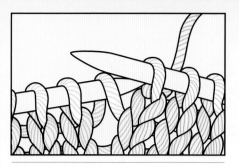

Figure 3

easy method that I often use for modular projects. Try this and see if you like the results.

Use a standard long-tail cast on. However, instead of casting on with a single needle, cast on with two needles held together, as shown in figure 1. This will double the size of each cast-on stitch and give all of the stitches even tension. After you have cast on the required number of stitches, gently slide one of the needles out of the stitches and begin the project. If the cast-on row is too loose and loopy for your liking, experiment by using a smaller needle with your cast-on needle.

KNITTED CAST ON

Because the concept of continuous knitting is that the modules grow, one of the most common methods for adding new modules is to use the knitted cast on. This method allows you to add new stitches to existing stitches.

To begin, insert the right-hand needle into the first stitch on the left-hand needle, as if to knit it. Knit the stitch, but do not drop the stitch from the left needle. Place the newly knitted stitch back on the left-hand needle (figure 2). Continue adding new

stitches in this manner until you have added as many stitches as the pattern calls for.

CLOSING HOLES

Most of the short rows in the diagonal knitting projects do not result in holes in the fabric. However, some of the short rows in the vertical and horizontal knitting projects may result in holes in the knitting. A good way to

prevent holes from forming is to make an extra stitch by pulling up the bar between the stitch you are knitting and the one you have just knitted. Add it to the left-hand needle, and instead of knitting the next stitch, knit the new stitch together with the next stitch to close the hole (figure 3). This has been abbreviated m1k1 wherever this technique is recommended.

BACKWARDS KNITTING

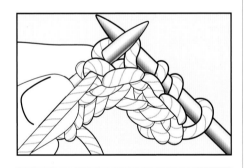

Figure 4

This is an optional technique that will speed up your modular knitting. Knitting backwards eliminates the need to turn your needles. It takes some practice, but is well worth the effort once you've mastered the technique.

Insert the left-hand needle under and up through the front of the first stitch

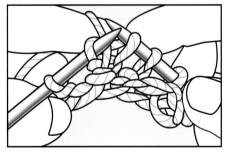

Figure 5

on the right-hand needle, as shown in figure 4. Wrap the yarn around the left-hand needle, bringing it around and letting it fall behind and between the left-hand and right-hand needles, and use the left-hand needle to pull down a loop with the new yarn (figure 5). Remove the old stitch from the right-hand needle (figure 6).

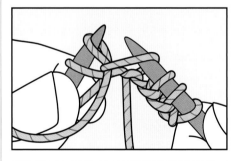

Figure 6

LOOSE BIND-OFF

Some projects require a loose bind-off. This is particularly true of the bigger projects with many stitches to bind-off. An easy method is to change to a larger set of needles for the bind-off row. Going up 2 or 3mm (one or two U.S. sizes) is generally sufficient. This will ensure that you are working the last stitches both evenly and loosely.

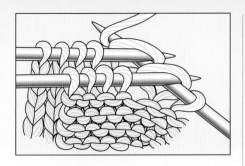

Figure 7

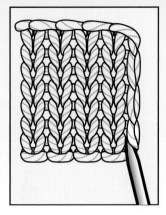

Figure 8

Figure 9

THREE-NEEDLE BIND-OFF

The three-needle bind-off is used to join two pieces together while binding off. This eliminates the need to sew seams.

With wrong sides of the knitted fabric facing outward, hold two needles together.

With a third needle, knit 2 stitches together: 1 stitch from the front needle and 1 stitch from the back needle. *K2tog again, taking 1 stitch from the front and 1 from the back. Pass the first stitch worked over the second as if

to bind off. Repeat from * until all stitches have been bound off (figure 7).

PICKING UP STITCHES

Some projects require that stitches be picked up from a bound-off or side-edge of a module. Insert the needle into both parts of the stitch in which you are picking up, and pull a loop through, as shown in figure 8. Pick up as many stitches as instructed in the pattern.

MAKING I-CORD

I-Cord is a knitted cord made on two double-pointed needles. To begin, cast 3 stitches onto a double-pointed needle. *Knit all stitches (figure 9). Do not turn. Slide the stitches to opposite end of the double-pointed needle. Repeat from * until the cord is the desired length. Bind off all stitches.

DESIGNING YOUR OWN

When you design your own projects, you must decide what modular knitting techniques to use. How do you decide when to use continuous knitting and when to use piecework knitting? The most important factor is the number of color and yarn changes in the project. It can also depend on your project size, number and size of modules, and how much flexibility you need in positioning the modules.

If you are working with more than two yarns, and the design is such that you will have to cut the yarn anyway, you may want to consider the piecework option. This option gives you unlimited flexibility in easily handling many different yarns—you can even make each module a different color combination. In the continuous method, stitches are not bound off and remain live on the needle. This could be a problem if you are developing a large project such as a blanket or afghan. In large proj-

ects with a lot of stitches on the needles, the heavy knitted fabric will pull on your needles and stretch the stitches out of shape, particularly with frequent turning for the short rows. For a large project you may prefer to use piecework knitting, because only the stitches from the current shape will be on your needles. The trade-off here is the ends to weave in versus the heavy needles.

If your work requires that you face the shapes in opposite directions, you will need to combine methods. For example, in the Building Blocks Shawl on page 61, you will knit each piece continuously, and sew the two pieces together later.

Finally, if your work is made up of many small modules, you'll probably appreciate the continuous knitting methods shown here. It would have been more difficult to knit the Square Holes Sweater on page 76 using the piecework method, considering that the project has over 300 unmitered squares!

GARTER STITCH SQUARES

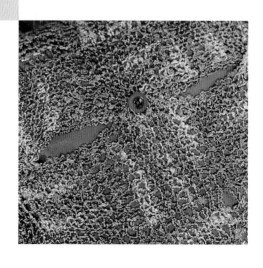

I N THIS CHAPTER, YOU WILL LEARN TO KNIT SQUARES IN A CONTINUOUS FASHION, BOTH VERTICALLY AND HORIZONTALLY. IN NO TIME AT ALL, YOU WILL FEEL COMFORTABLE KNITTING SQUARES IN ALTERNATING DIRECTIONS.

SHAPES TO LEARN

Figure 1:

1 VERTICAL SIDE SQUARE

2 HORIZONTAL MIDDLE SQUARE

3 VERTICAL MIDDLE SQUARE

4 HORIZONTAL SIDE SQUARE

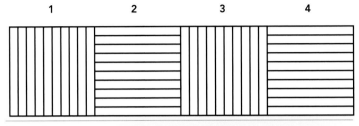

Figure 1

■ VERTICAL AND HORIZONTAL SIDE SQUARES

In this simple exercise, you will make a swatch with 5 stitch by 5 row vertical and horizontal squares, as shown in figure 2.

Cast on 10 stitches.

Step 1

Make a Vertical Side Square.

Using the knitted cast on, CO 5 more stitches.

Row 1: K1inc1, k3, skp, turn; s1, k4—1 st left unknitted—turn.

Repeat row 1 leaving 1 additional st unknitted in every repetition until there are 4 sts left unknitted. Don't forget to turn.

K1inc1, k3, skp, *do not turn*—10 sts on right needle, 5 sts on left needle.

Step 2

Create an attached Horizontal Side Square.

Row 1: K5, turn.

Row 2: K4, skp, turn; s1, k4, turn.

Repeat row 2 a total of 5 times to complete first set of squares—10 sts.

Repeat steps 1 and 2 to create a second set of squares. The vertical square is above the first horizontal square and the horizontal square is above the first vertical square (see figure 2).

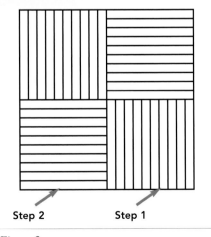

Step 2   Step 1

Figure 2

■ Four Alternating Squares

In this exercise you will learn how to knit multiple repetitions of vertical and horizontal squares in a single row, as shown in figure 3.

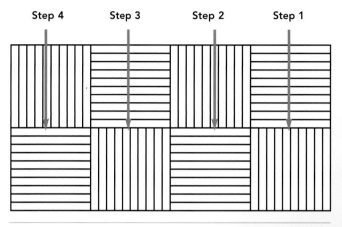

Figure 3

Cast on 20 sts.

Step 1

Make a Vertical Side Square.

Note: This is the same as Step 1 of Exercise 1.

Using the knitted cast on, CO 5 more stitches.

TIP: *For a smoother edge, cast on 21 sts and add 4 sts with the knitted cast on the first time you begin Step 1.*

Row 1: K1inc1, k3, skp, turn; s1, k4—1 st left unknitted—turn.

Repeat row 1 leaving 1 additional st unknitted in every repetition until there are 4 sts left unknitted. Turn. K1inc1, k3, skp, do not turn—10 sts on right needle, 15 sts on left needle.

Step 2

Create an attached Horizontal Middle Square.

Row 1: K5, turn (this creates a gap).

Row 2: K1inc1, k3, skp, turn; s1, k4—1 st left unknitted before the gap—turn.

Repeat row 2 four more times, leaving an extra st unknitted each time until there are 5 sts left unknitted before the gap, *do not turn.*

Step 3

Create an attached Vertical Middle Square.

Row 1: K1inc1, k3, skp, turn; s1, k4—1 st left unknitted—turn.

Repeat row 1 a total of 4 times until there are 4 sts left unknitted. Don't forget to turn.

K1inc1, k3, skp, *do not turn.*

Step 4

Create an attached Horizontal Side Square.

Note: This is the same as Step 2 of Exercise 1.

Row 1: K5, turn.

Row 2: K4, skp, turn; s1, k4, turn.

Repeat row 2 a total of 5 times to complete first set of squares—20 sts.

The first set of squares is now complete. Repeat steps 1 to 4 to stack a second set of squares above the first set, as shown in figure 3.

EXPANDING THESE TECHNIQUES

If you understand how this works, you can adapt the technique to any knitted item.

For vertical squares:

1. Increase each row with a k1inc1 on one side.

2. Knit to the last stitch.

3. Skp to connect the last stitch with the cast-on row or the base row.

For horizontal squares:

1. Knit across each row.

2. Turn and knit to the last st.

3. Skp to attach the last st to the corresponding row in the vertical square just completed.

Note the differences between your two practice swatches.

■ While creating a Horizontal Middle Square, a k1inc1 is added to the newly formed side of each square to create the extra stitches needed to attach the next Vertical Square.

■ In both swatches, the Horizontal Square is attached to the corresponding rows of the previously formed Vertical Square with a skp.

■ The only change in the Middle Vertical Square is that no knitted cast on is required.

PATCHWORK EYEGLASS CASE

THIS SMALL EYEGLASS CASE SHOWS OFF THE BEAUTIFUL COLORS AND SHEEN OF THE SILK YARN. EASY ENOUGH TO KNIT IN A WEEKEND, IT MAKES A PERFECT LAST-MINUTE GIFT. BUY AN EXTRA BALL OF YARN, BECAUSE YOU'LL WANT TO MAKE ONE FOR YOURSELF!

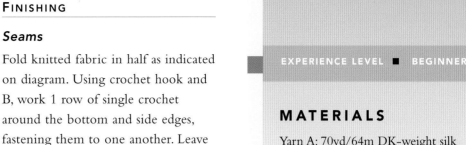

INSTRUCTIONS

Cast on 30 sts.

Step 1

Make the first row of Squares.

Square 1 (Horizontal): *K5, turn; k1inc1, k4, turn. Rep from * 5 times—0, 1, 2, 3, 4 sts left unknitted. K5, *do not turn*—5 sts unknitted.

Square 2 (Vertical): *K1inc1, k3, skp, turn; s1, k4, turn; rep from * 4 times. K1inc1, k3, skp, *do not turn*.

Square 3 (Horizontal): K5, turn; *k1inc1, k3, skp, turn; s1, k4, turn (1, 2, 3, 4, 5 sts left unknitted); rep from * 5 times, *do not turn*.

Square 4 (Vertical): Repeat Square 2.

Square 5 (Horizontal): Repeat Square 3.

Square 6 (Vertical): *K1inc1, k3, skp, turn; s1, k4, turn; rep from * 4 times. K1inc1, k3, skp. Bind off 5 sts—30 sts.

Steps 2 to 6

Make five more rows of Squares.

Repeat instructions in Step 1.

Bind off all sts. Cut yarn.

FINISHING

Seams

Fold knitted fabric in half as indicated on diagram. Using crochet hook and B, work 1 row of single crochet around the bottom and side edges, fastening them to one another. Leave top open and work 1 round of single crochet around opening.

Button Loop

Using crochet hook and A, attach A to top of case in position to fasten button. Chain 26 sts. Fasten stitch 26 to stitch 9 with a single crochet. Chain 9. Attach A to top of case, making a figure 8 shape.

Sew button to other side of case in position so that end loop of figure 8 chain fits around button securely.

Cut yarn. Weave in ends.

THIS EYEGLASS CASE WAS KNIT WITH:

(A) 1 SKEIN ALCHEMY'S SILK PURSE, 100% SILK, 1.8OZ/50G = 138YD/126M, COLOR #57M HEART

(B) 1 SKEIN LANG'S BACCARA, 85% SILK/15% NYLON, 1.8OZ/50G = 143YD/131M PER BALL, COLOR PINK

Step 6
Step 5
Step 4
- - Fold Here
Step 3
Step 2
Step 1

MATERIALS

Yarn A: 70yd/64m DK-weight silk yarn that knits up at 21 sts per 4"/10cm

Yarn B: 10yd/9m worsted-weight fur yarn

Knitting needles: 4mm (size 6 U.S.) *or size to obtain gauge*

Crochet hook: 3.5mm (size E U.S.)

One ½"/1.3cm round wooden button

Sewing needle and matching thread

FINISHED MEASUREMENTS

3¾"/9.5cm wide x 7"/17.8cm long

GAUGE

5 sts x 5 row square = 1"/2.5cm in Pattern Stitch

Always take time to check your gauge.

PATTERN STITCH

VERTICAL AND HORIZONTAL GARTER STITCH SQUARES

See page 20, and make a small practice swatch if you have never used this technique before.

ADE WITH ONLY HORIZONTAL AND VERTICAL RECTANGLES, THESE GORGEOUS PILLOWS ARE AN EXCELLENT INTRODUCTION TO SEAMLESS MODULAR KNITTING. THE SPLASH OF FUR AROUND THE EDGES ADDS JUST THE RIGHT AMOUNT OF FLAIR.

BASKETWEAVE PILLOW

Vertical & Horizontal Garter Stitch Squares

INSTRUCTIONS

Cast on 40 sts.

Step 1

Make first row of Squares.

Horizontal Square 1: K8, turn; *k1inc1, k7, turn; k8, turn; rep from * a total of 7 times—1, 2, 3, 4, 5, 6, 7 sts left unknitted. K1inc1, k7, turn; k8, *do not turn*—8 sts unknitted.

Square 2: *K1inc1, k6, skp, turn; s1, k7, turn; rep from * a total of 7 times. K1inc1, k6, skp, *do not turn.*

Square 3: K8, turn; *k1inc1, k6, skp, turn; s1, k7, turn; rep from * a total of 7 times. K1inc1, k6, skp, turn; s1, k7, *do not turn.*

Square 4: Repeat Square 2.

Square 5: K8, turn; *k7, skp, turn; s1, k7, turn; rep from * a total of 8 times—40 sts.

Step 2

Make second row of Squares.

Using the knitted cast on, CO an additional 8 sts and turn.

Square 1: *K1inc1, k6, skp, turn; s1, k7, turn; rep from * a total of 7 times. End with k1inc1, k6, skp, *do not turn.*

Squares 2 and 4: Repeat Square 3 of Step 1.

Square 3: Repeat Square 2 of Step 1.

*K1inc1, k6, skp, turn; s1, k7, turn; rep from * a total of 7 times. End with k1inc1, k6, skp, turn; bind off 8 sts.

Steps 3 to 8

Repeat Steps 1 and 2 three more times, adding a buttonhole the last time you work Step 2.

Modify Square 3 to add a buttonhole as follows: *K1inc1, k6, skp, turn; s1, k7, turn; rep from * a total of 3 times. K1inc1, yo, k2tog, k4, skp, turn; s1, k7, turn. *K1inc1, k6, skp, turn; s1, k7, turn; rep from * a total of 3 times. End with k1inc1, k6, skp, *do not turn.*

FINISHING

Fold knitted piece as indicated in the diagram. Turn wrong side out and sew side seams. Turn right side out and insert pillow form. Position button so it fits into buttonhole, and sew it on. Using a crochet hook and B, work several rows of single crochet around all four pillow sides.

Cut yarn, weave in ends.

THIS PILLOW WAS KNIT WITH:

(A) 1 HANK OF FIESTA'S RAYON BOUCLE, 100% RAYON, 4OZ/113G = APPROX 225YD/206M PER HANK, COLOR CATALINA

(B) 1 BALL OF HABU TEXTILES' POLY MOIRE, 100% POLYESTER EYELASH YARN, 0.5 OZ/14G = APPROX 23YD/21M PER BALL, COLOR 24 BEIGE

MATERIALS

Yarn A: 200yd/183m worsted-weight yarn that knits up at 20 sts to 4"/10cm

Yarn B: 20yd/18.3m fur or eyelash yarn for trim

Knitting needles: 5.5mm (size 9 U.S.) *or size to obtain gauge*

Crochet hook: 3.5mm (size E U.S.)

One ¹⁄₂"/1.3cm button

Sewing needle and matching thread

12"/30.5cm square pillow form

FINISHED MEASUREMENTS

12"/30.5cm square

GAUGE

8 st x 16 row square = 3¹⁄₂"/8.9cm in Pattern Stitch

Always take time to check your gauge.

PATTERN STITCH

VERTICAL AND HORIZONTAL GARTER STITCH SQUARES

See page 20, and make a small practice swatch if you have never used this technique before.

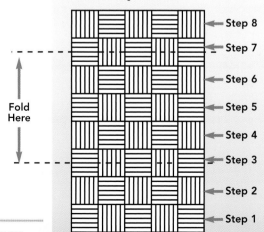

TRIANGLES
AND
DIAMONDS

I N THIS CHAPTER, YOU WILL LEARN TO KNIT TRIAN- GLES AND DIAMONDS ON THE DIAGONAL IN A CONTINUOUS FASHION.

SHAPES TO LEARN

Note: Practice Practice both swatches, making note of two consistent practices in this technique:

- K1inc1 is always used for the increase.

- Skp is always used for the decrease.

It is important to identify the location for the next increase and decrease. These are consistent for every shape. Once you can recognize where to increase and decrease, you will be able to follow the directions in the projects without needing stitch markers.

The decrease always closes the gap between the previous row's slipped stitch and the shape to which the new shape is being joined. Skp, slipping the last stitch before the gap and knitting the first stitch after the gap.

Figure 1:

1 RIGHT TRIANGLE BEGINNING

2 SIDE EQUILATERAL TRIANGLE

3 RIGHT TRIANGLE ENDING

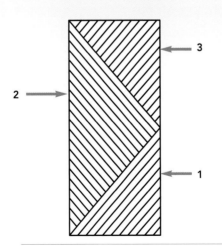

Figure 1

Figure 2:

4 UPRIGHT EQUILATERAL TRIANGLE BEGINNING

5 DIAMOND

6 UPRIGHT EQUILATERAL TRIANGLE ENDING

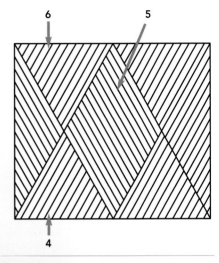

Figure 2

■ DIAGONAL TRIANGLES

In this exercise, you will practice making diagonal triangles.

Cast on 5 sts.

Step 1

Make a Right Triangle Beginning.

Row 1: K1inc1, k1, turn; s1, k to end, turn—3 sts worked.

Note: There are more than 3 sts on the needles. The reference to the number of sts always indicates the number of "live" sts that have already been worked in the shape.

Row 2: K1inc1, k3, turn; s1, k to end, turn—5 sts.

Row 3: K1inc1, k5, turn; s1, k to end, turn—7 sts.

Row 4: K1inc1, k7—9 sts.

Note: You end with twice the number of cast-on stitches minus 1.

Step 2

Make a Side Equilateral Triangle.

Start this triangle at the bottommost part of the Right Triangle Beginning.

Row 1: K1inc1, skp, turn; s1, k to end, turn—3 sts.

Row 2: K1inc1, k1, skp, turn; s1, k to end, turn—4 sts.

Row 3: K1inc1, k2, skp, turn; s1, k to end, turn—5 sts.

Row 4: K1inc1, k3, skp, turn; s1, k to end, turn—6 sts.

Row 5: K1inc1, k4, skp, turn; s1, k to end, turn—7 sts.

Row 6: K1inc1, k5, skp, turn; s1, k to end, turn—8 sts.

Row 7: K1inc1, k6, skp, turn—9 sts.

Step 3

Make a Right Triangle Ending.

Rows 1 to 3: Repeat rows 1 to 3 of Step 2.

Row 4: S1, k3, skp, turn; s1, k3, turn—1 st left unknitted.

Row 5: S1, pass 2nd st on right needle over 1st, k2, skp, turn; s1, k2, turn—1 st unknitted.

Row 6: S1, pass 2nd st on right needle over 1st, k1, skp, turn; s1, k1, turn—1 st unknitted.

Row 7: S1, pass 2nd st on right needle over 1st, skp, pass 2nd st on right needle over 1st.

Fasten off last st.

Note: Start binding off stitches (as instructed in rows 4 to 7 above) when the number of knitted stitches of the end triangle equals the number of cast-on stitches (in this exercise, 5 stitches).

■ UPRIGHT TRIANGLES AND DIAMONDS

Cast on 10 sts.

Step 1

Make two Upright Equilateral Triangles (5 x 5 x 5 sts each).

Row 1: K1inc1, turn; s1, turn—1 st left unknitted.

Row 2: K1inc1, k1, turn; s1, k1, turn—2 sts left unknitted.

Row 3: K1inc1, k2, turn; s1, k2, turn—3 sts left unknitted.

Row 4: K1inc1, k3, turn; s1, k3, turn—4 sts left unknitted.

Row 5: K1inc1, k4, *do not turn.*

Repeat rows 1 to 5 to create a second Upright Equilateral Triangle. Turn.

Step 2

Make a Side Equilateral Triangle.

Row 1: K1inc1, skp, turn; s1, k2, turn—3 sts.

Row 2: K1inc1, k1, skp, turn; s1, k3, turn—4 sts.

Row 3: K1inc1, k2, skp, *do not turn*—5 sts.

Step 3

Make a Diamond.

Row 1: K1inc1, k3, skp, turn; s1, k4, turn—1 st left unknitted.

Row 2: K1inc1, k3, skp, turn; s1, k4, turn—2 sts left unknitted.

Row 3: K1inc1, k3, skp, turn; s1, k4, turn—3 sts left unknitted.

Row 4: K1inc1, k3, skp, turn; s1, k4, turn—4 sts left unknitted.

Row 5: K1inc1, k3, skp, *do not turn.*

Check your work. There should be 15 sts on the right needle and 5 sts on the left needle.

Step 4

Make a Side Equilateral Triangle facing the opposite side.

K5, turn (position at bottom of Upright Equilateral Triangle).

Repeat rows 1 and 2 of Step 2.

Row 3: K1inc1, k2, skp, turn; s1, k4.

Step 5

Make two Upright Equilateral Ending Triangles.

First Upright Equilateral Ending Triangle:

Row 1: K4, skp, turn; s1, k3, turn—1 st unknitted.

Row 2: S1, pass 2nd st on right needle over 1st, k2, skp, turn; s1, k2, turn—1 st unknitted.

Row 3: S1, pass 2nd st on right needle over 1st, k1, skp, turn; s1, k1, turn—1 st unknitted.

(continued on next page)

Row 4: S1, pass 2nd st on right needle over 1st, skp, pass 2nd st on right needle over 1st, k1, pass 2nd st on right needle over 1st—1 st remains on right needle, 10 sts remain on left needle.

Second Upright Equilateral Ending Triangle:

Row 1: K1, pass 2nd st on right needle over 1st, k3, skp, turn; s1, k3, turn—1 st unknitted.

Row 2: S1, pass 2nd st on right needle over 1st, k2, skp, turn; s1, k2, turn—1 st unknitted.

Row 3: S1, pass 2nd st on right needle over 1st, k1, skp, turn; s1, k1, turn—1 st unknitted.

Row 4: S1, pass 2nd st on right needle over 1st, skp, pass 2nd st on right needle over 1st, k1, pass 2nd st on right needle over 1st. Fasten off last st.

NOTES ON KNITTING DIAGONAL TRIANGLES AND DIAMONDS

Right diagonal triangles are formed by increasing on both ends—on the right side with a k1inc1 and on the left side by picking up an extra stitch from the base, or cast-on, row.

Side equilateral triangles are formed by increasing on the side and joining with a skp to the previous triangle. As in the right diagonal triangles, the increase is on the right side with a k1inc1. The join is on the left side and con-nects the last stitch of the side equilateral triangle with the previous triangle's stitch, using the skp to connect the two (making 1 stitch out of 2 stitches).

Diamonds and equilateral upright triangles are formed similarly. Even though the knitting is on the diagonal, the increases take place from the top of the triangle or diamond. The join, as before, is with the skp, and connects the current shape with the previous shape.

MULTI-DIRECTIONAL SCARF

HIS ATTRACTIVE SCARF WORKS AS WELL WITH BRIGHT COLORS AS WITH BLACK AND GRAY YARNS. MADE WITH SIMPLE TRIANGLES, THE ADDITION OF COLOR CHANGES AND STRIPES KEEPS THE KNITTING INTERESTING. THE UNUSUAL CONSTRUCTION INVOLVES WORKING TWO COLORS WITHOUT EVER HAVING TO CUT EITHER YARN FROM BEGINNING TO END.

MATERIALS

Approx total: 300 yd/274.3m worsted-weight yarn that knits up at 20 sts to 4"/10cm

Color A: 150 yd/137.2m in green

Color B: 150 yd/137.2m in blue

Approx total: 50 yd/45.7m silk ribbon yarn for fringe

Color C: 25 yd/22.9m in green

Color D: 25 yd/22.9m in blue

Knitting needles: 5mm (size 8 U.S.) circular needle *or size to obtain gauge*

Crochet hook: 3.5mm (size E U.S.)

Stitch marker

FINISHED MEASUREMENTS

Approx 54"/137.2cm x 4¼"/10.8cm without fringe

GAUGE

16 sts and 34 rows = 4"/10cm in Garter Stitch

Always take time to check your gauge.

PATTERN STITCHES

DIAGONAL TRIANGLES
See page 28, and make a small practice swatch if you have never used this technique before.

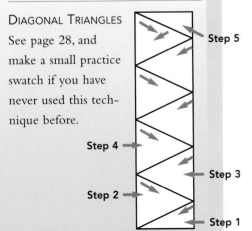

Step 5
Step 4
Step 3
Step 2
Step 1

INSTRUCTIONS

Loosely cast on 16 sts.

Note: You can easily make this scarf any size. To make the scarf wider, cast on more stitches; to make it narrower, cast on fewer sts. When the first triangle is complete, the number of stitches on the needle should be twice the number of cast-on stitches, less 1 stitch.

Step 1

Make Right Triangle (in A).

Row 1: With A, k1inc1, k1, turn; s1, k to end, turn.

Row 2: K1inc1, k3, turn; pm, s1, k to end, turn.

Row 3: K1inc1, k to marker, rm, k1, turn; pm, s1, k to end, turn.

Repeat row 3 until all cast-on sts have been used and there are 31 sts in total. Color A will be positioned at the top of the triangle. Slide all sts to other side of needle and attach B. Do not cut A.

Step 2

Make first Equilateral Triangle (in B).

Row 1: With B, k1inc1, skp, turn; s1, k to end, turn.

Row 2: K1inc1, k1, skp, turn; s1, pm, k to end, turn.

Row 3: K1inc1, k to marker, rm, skp, turn; s1, pm, k to end, turn.

Repeat row 3, until you have used up all but one of the previous triangle's sts. End with: k1inc1, k to marker, rm, skp—31 sts. B is positioned at the lower point of the 2nd triangle.

Step 3

Make second Equilateral Triangle (in A and B Stripes).

Row 1: With A, k1inc1, skp, turn; s1, k to end, drop A, turn.

Row 2: With B, k1inc1, k1, skp, turn; s1, pm, k to end, drop B, turn.

Row 3: With A, k1inc1, k to marker, rm, skp, turn; s1, pm, k to end, turn.

Repeat row 3, alternating A and B, making sure that A is at the lower point of the triangle in position to turn and knit the fourth triangle, and

B is at the upper point of the triangle when you have used up all the 2nd Triangle sts—31 sts.

Step 4

Make third Equilateral Triangle (in A).

Repeat instructions for Step 2, substituting A for B. When A is used, last row should end as follows: With A, k1incl1, k to marker, rm, skp, turn; k to end. Slide all sts to other side of needle and start knitting with B. Do not cut A. Turn.

Repeat Steps 2 to 4 until 11 triangles are complete, or until scarf is desired length.

Step 5

Make End Triangle (in A).

Note: If you changed the length of the scarf, use the appropriate color for this triangle.

Row 1: K1inc1, skp, turn; s1, k to end, turn.

Row 2: K1inc1, k1, pm, skp, turn; s1, pm, k to end, turn.

Row 3: K1inc1, k to marker, rm, skp, turn; s1, pm, k to end, turn.

Repeat row 3 until all but 15 sts of the previous triangle's sts have been used up (half less one stitch), and then continue as follows:

Row 1: Skp, k to marker, rm, skp, turn; s1, pm, k to last 1 st, turn—1 st left unknitted on the right needle.

Row 2: S1, pass 2nd st on right needle over 1st, k to marker, rm, skp, turn; s1, pm, k to last 1 st, turn.

Repeat row 2 until a total of 3 sts remain.

Bind off rem sts.

FINISHING

Cut yarn. Weave in ends.

Attach Fringe

Cut thirty-six 15"/38.1cm lengths of silk ribbon, color C, and thirty-six 15"/38.1cm lengths of silk ribbon, color D.

Each fringe requires 3 lengths of color C and 3 lengths of color D. Using crochet hook, pull 6 strand loop through bottom stitch on scarf edge, and knot the fringe by passing the strands through the loop. Make 6 evenly spaced fringes on each end of scarf. Trim fringes to even them out.

THIS PROJECT WAS KNIT WITH:

(A) 1 SKEIN ARTYARNS ULTRAMERINO 8, 3 1/2OZ/100G=188YD/169.2M PER SKEIN, COLOR #118 GREEN

(B) 1 SKEIN ARTYARNS ULTRAMERINO 8, 3 1/2OZ/100G = 188 YD/169.2M PER SKEIN, COLOR #121 BLUE

THE FRINGE WAS MADE WITH:

(C) 1 SKEIN ARTYARNS SILK RIBBON, .9OZ/25G = 128YD/115.2M PER SKEIN, COLOR #118 GREEN

(D) 1 SKEIN ARTYARNS SILK RIBBON, .9OZ/25G = 128YD/115.2M PER SKEIN, COLOR #121 BLUE

STARBURST SHAWL

EQUALLY SUITED FOR A NIGHT ON THE TOWN OR A SUNDAY BRUNCH, THIS AIRY SHAWL WILL BECOME A STAPLE IN YOUR WARDROBE AS SOON AS YOU TAKE IT OFF THE NEEDLES. GARTER STITCH DIAMONDS SURROUNDED BY OPENWORK PANELS SHOW OFF THE LUSTER AND DRAPE OF THE SILK YARN, AND THE SMALL SIZE MAKES THIS SHAWL COMFORTABLE AND VERSATILE.

MATERIALS

Approx total: 500yd/457m worsted-weight silk yarn that knits up at 20 sts to 4"/10cm

Knitting needles: 5mm (size 8 U.S.) *or size to obtain gauge*

FINISHED MEASUREMENTS

Approx 13"/33cm wide x 52"/132cm long

GAUGE

8 st x 8 row diamond = 2"/5cm in Pattern Stitch

Always take time to check your gauge.

PATTERN STITCHES

UPRIGHT TRIANGLES AND DIAMONDS See page 29, and make a small practice swatch if you have never used these techniques before.

OPENWORK PARTITION

Work a yo between each stitch working k1inc1 as follows: knit in front of st, knit in back of st, yo.

On the next row, drop the yarn over to create elongated stitches.

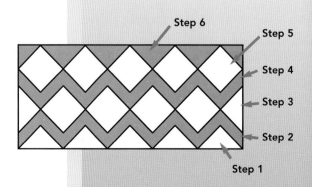

Step 6
Step 5
Step 4
Step 3
Step 2
Step 1

INSTRUCTIONS

Cast on 40 sts.

Note: For a wider shawl, cast on additional sts in multiples of 8.

Step 1

Make 5 Upright Beginning Triangles for bottom of shawl.

Triangle 1:

Row 1: K1inc1, turn; s1, turn.

Row 2: K1inc1, k1, turn; s1, k1, turn.

Row 3: K1inc1, k2, turn; s1, k2, turn.

Row 4: K1inc1, k3, turn; s1, k3, turn.

Row 5: K1inc1, k4, turn; s1, k4, turn.

Row 6: K1inc1, k5, turn; s1, k5, turn.

Row 7: K1inc1, k6, turn; s1, k6, turn.

Row 8: K1inc1, k7—16 sts, *do not turn*.

Triangles 2 to 5: Repeat rows 1 to 8 four more times—32, 48, 64, 80 sts. Turn.

Step 2

Make Openwork Partition 1, working across all sts.

Row 1: K1, yo, ★(k1, yo) 6 times, k1inc1, yo, (k1, yo) 7 times, k2tog, yo; repeat from ★ 3 times, (k1,yo) 6 times, k1inc1, yo, (k1,yo) 6 times, k2tog.

Row 2: Dropping each yarn over across row, ★k7, k1inc1, k6, k2tog; repeat from ★ to end—80 sts.

Step 3

Make Pattern Design 1.

Side Triangle 1:

Row 1: K1inc1, skp, turn; s1, k2, turn.

Row 2: K1inc1, k1, skp, turn; s1, k3, turn.

Row 3: K1inc1, k2, skp, turn; s1, k4, turn.

Row 4: K1inc1, k3, skp, turn; s1, k5, turn.

Row 5: K1inc1, k4, skp, turn; s1, k6, turn.

Row 6: K1inc1, k5, skp, , *do not turn*.

Diamond 1:

Row 1: K1inc1, k6, skp, turn; s1, k7, turn.

Repeat row 1 six more times, then end with k1inc1, k6, skp, *do not turn*.

Diamonds 2 to 4:

Repeat Diamond 1.

Side Triangle 2:

Row 1: K8 (end of row—80 sts on needles); turn.

Rows 2-6: Repeat rows 1 to 5 of Side Triangle 1 in Step 3.

Row 7: K1inc1, k5, skp, turn; s1, k7, turn.

Step 4

Make Openwork Partition 2, working across all sts.

Row 1: K1inc1, yo, (k1,yo) 6 times, ★k2tog, yo, (k1,yo) 6 times, k1inc1, yo, (k1,yo) 7 times; rep from ★ to last 9 sts, k2tog, yo, (k1,yo) 6 times, k1.

Row 2: K1inc1, k6, ★k2tog, k6, k1inc1, k7; rep from ★ to last 9 sts, k2tog, k7—80 stitches

Step 5

Make Pattern Design 2.

Diamond 1:

Row 1: K1inc1, k6, skp, turn; s1, k7, turn.

Repeat row 1 six more times. Then end with K1inc1, k6, skp, *do not turn*.

Diamonds 2 to 5:

Repeat Diamond 1.

Repeat Steps 2 to 5 ten more times, or until shawl is desired length. End with Step 4.

Step 6

Make 5 Upright Ending Triangles for top of shawl.

Row 1: K7, skp, turn; s1, k7, turn.

Row 2: S1, k6, skp, turn; s1, k6, s1wyif, turn.

Row 3: S2psso, k5, skp, turn; s1, k5, s1wyif, turn.

Row 4: S2psso, k4, skp, turn; s1, k4, s1wyif, turn.

Row 5: S2psso, k3, skp, turn; s1, k3, s1wyif, turn.

Row 6: S2psso, k2, skp, turn; s1, k2, s1wyif, turn.

Row 7: S2psso, k1, skp, turn; s1, k1, s1wyif, turn.

Row 8: S2psso, skp, bind off 2 times across 3 sts—64 sts rem.

Row 9: K6, skp, turn; s1, k6, s1wyif, turn

Repeat rows 2 to 9 three more times and then rows 2 to 8 one time until 1 st rem.

FINISHING

Cut yarn, pull yarn through last stitch, and weave in ends.

THIS SHAWL WAS KNIT WITH:

4 SKEINS OF ALCHEMY'S SILK PURSE, 100% SILK, APPROX 1.8OZ/50G = 138YD/126M PER SKEIN, COLOR FIRE AND ICE

Diagonal Triangles and Diamonds

FELTED GEOMETRIC TOTE

WHAT COULD BE MORE FUN AND USEFUL THAN THIS FELTED PURSE? YOU KNIT AT A LOOSE GAUGE ON LARGE NEEDLES, SO THE KNITTING GOES QUICKLY. WHEN YOU'RE FINISHED, YOU THROW THE BAG IN THE WASHING MACHINE AND SHRINK IT TO SIZE. THE LOOSELY KNIT STITCHES QUICKLY TURN INTO A DENSE, STURDY FABRIC AND THE BRIGHT COLORS OF THE YARN BLEND TOGETHER TO CREATE A MUTED PALETTE THAT WILL COMPLEMENT ANY WARDROBE.

MATERIALS

Approx Total: 300 yards worsted-weight 100% wool yarn that knits up at 20 sts to 4"/10cm

Note: Choose yarn that will felt—only non-washable 100% wool yarns will be suitable for this project.

Knitting needles: Size 5mm (size 8 U.S.) 24"/61cm circular needles *or size to obtain gauge*

Extra knitting needle for three-needle bind-off

Sewing needle and matching thread

Washing machine and mesh laundry bag with zipper for felting

2"/5cm pendant or button to fasten

FINISHED MEASUREMENTS

Approx 10"/25.4cm wide x 10"/25.4cm long after felting. Strap is 30"/76.2cm long, fastener is 11½"/29.2cm long.

Note: This bag is worked at a loose gauge, then washed in the washing machine several times until it shrinks and is felted. The exact size is determined during felting.

GAUGE

8 stitch x 16 row Diamond = 2"/5cm x 2"/5cm before felting
Always take time to check your gauge.

(Pattern Stitch is described on page 40.)

Diagonal Triangles and Diamonds

PATTERN STITCHES

DIAGONAL TRIANGLES AND DIAMONDS

See page 28, and make a small practice swatch if you have never used this technique before.

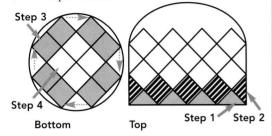

Bottom   **Top**

Note: Dotted arrows represent joined sides (joined with skps)

INSTRUCTIONS

Note: Bag is knitted from top to bottom and knit in-the-round. The bag is symmetrically shaped because of its construction. To make a longer purse, repeat Step 2 until you have reached your desired length. Don't forget that the bag will shrink when you felt it.

Cast on 64 sts.

Step 1

Make 8 Base Triangles for top of bag.

Triangle 1:

Row 1: K1inc1, turn; s1, turn.

Row 2: k1inc1, k1, turn; s1, k1 turn.

Row 3: K1inc1, k2, turn; s1, k2 turn.

Row 4: K1inc1, k3, turn; s1, k3 turn.

Row 5: K1inc1, k4, turn; s1, k4 turn.

Row 6: K1inc1, k5, turn; s1, k5 turn.

Row 7: K1inc1, k6, turn; s1, k6 turn.

Row 8: K1inc1, k7, *do not turn*—16 sts.

Triangles 2 to 8: Repeat rows 1 to 8.

You will have 16 more sts after each

triangle—32, 48, 64, 80, 96, 112, 128 sts. After 8 triangles are complete, you should have 128 stitches on the needles. Join and work in-the-round.

Step 2

Make the bag body.

Diamond 1:

K8. This puts you in the correct location to start knitting the next row of diamonds.

Row 1: *K1inc1, k6, skp, turn; s1, k7, turn; repeat from * a total of 7 times. K1inc1, k6, skp, *do not turn*. (Count the stitches on the top of your diamond—there should be 8 on one side and 8 on the other.)

Diamonds 2 to 8:

Repeat row 1 seven more times.

Repeat instructions for Diamonds 1 to 8 a total of 4 times to create 4 rounds of diamonds. If you would like a longer bag, add more rounds.

Step 3

Work decrease round to turn the 8 diamonds into 4 pairs of diamonds (see diagram). K8. This puts you in the correct location to start knitting the next row of diamonds.

Diamond 1 (first Diamond of Pair):

*K1inc1, k6, skp, turn; s1, k7, turn; repeat from * 6 more times for a total of 7 times. K1inc1, k6, skp, do not turn. (Count the stitches on the top of your diamond. There should be 8 on one side and 8 on the other.)

Diamond 2 (second Diamond of Pair):

K1, k6, skp, turn; *s1, k6, skp, turn;

repeat from * 14 more times for a total of 15 times. S1, k7.

Create two more pairs of diamonds by repeating Diamonds 1 and 2 two more times. End round by repeating Diamond 1, and then replacing Diamond 2 with the following:

K7, skp, turn. *S1, k6, skp, turn; repeat from * 15 more times for a total of 16 times—64 sts.

Step 4

Work the final decrease round to decrease from 8 to 4 diamonds, and join them to form a square.

Diamond 1:

*K1inc1, k6, skp, turn; s1, k7, turn; repeat from * a total of 7 times. K1inc1, k6, skp, *do not turn*. (Count the stitches on the top of your diamond. There should be 8 on one side and 8 on the other.) Put the 8 stitches on the top right side of the diamond just knitted on a stitch holder.

Diamond 2:

K1, k6, skp, turn; *s1, k6, skp, turn; repeat from * a total of 16 times.

Diamonds 3 and 4:

Repeat Diamond 2 twice—8 stitches remain.

Step 5

Attach the 8 stitches from Diamond 1 to the 8 stitches from Diamond 4.

Turn the bag inside out. Take 8 sts off the stitch holder and put them on the extra knitting needle. Use the three-needle bind-off to seamlessly attach these last two sets of 8 stitches.

Cut yarn.

Step 6

Make the strap.

Cast on 5 sts.

Row 1: K1inc1, k1, turn; s1, k to end, turn—3sts.

Row 2: K1inc1, k3, turn; s1, k to end, turn—5 sts.

Row 3: K1inc1, k5, turn; s1, k to end, turn—7 sts.

Row 4: K1inc1, k7; turn—9 sts.

Row 5 (begin equilateral triangle): K1inc1, skp, turn; s1, k to end, turn—3 sts.

Row 6: K1inc1, k1, skp, turn; s1, k to end, turn—4 sts.

Row 7: K1inc1, k2, skp, turn; s1, k to end, turn—5 sts.

Row 8: K1inc1, k3, skp, turn; s1, k to end, turn—6 sts.

Row 9: K1inc1, k4, skp, turn; s1, k to end, turn—7 sts.

Row 10: K1inc1, k5, skp, turn; s1, k to end, turn—8 sts.

Row 11: K1inc1, k6, skp; turn—9 sts.

Repeat rows 5 to 11 until strap is at 52"/132cm or desired length, making an allowance for the felting shrinkage.

End the strap as follows:

Rows 1 to 3: Repeat rows 5 to 7.

Row 4: S1, k3, skp, turn; s1, k3, turn—1 st left unknitted.

Row 5: S1, pass 2nd st on right needle over 1st, k2, skp, turn; s1, k2, turn.

Row 6: S1, pass 2nd st on right needle over 1st, k1, skp, turn; s1, k1, turn.

Row 7: S1, pass 2nd st on right needle over 1st, skp, bo 2 sts.

Cut yarn.

FINISHING

Weave in ends.

Felting

Place bag and strap into mesh laundry bag, zip it closed, and put it in regular washing machine with a small amount of soap. Set the machine for hot water. Expect to run it through the cycle three or four times, until it is completely felted. If desired, add a pair of old jeans for extra agitation to speed up the felting process. Hang bag and strap to dry.

Construction

Cut approx 11½"/29.2cm of felt from the strap to use for the latch. Sew pendant or button in position in the center of the bag approximately 3"/7.6cm below rim. Sew felted latch in loop position to secure button on the opposite side of the bag, as shown in the illustration. Sew one end of the strap to one side of the bag, and the other end to the opposite side. Cut all yarn. Weave in ends.

THIS BAG WAS KNIT WITH:

3 SKEINS OF NORO'S KUREYO PATORA, 100% WOOL, APPROX 1.8OZ/50G = 120YD/110M PER SKEIN, IN COLOR #5

Flat-Top Hat

THIS CUTE CLOCHE IS KNIT IN-THE-ROUND WITH ALTERNATING KNIT AND PURL ROWS FORMING GARTER STITCH ON THE BRIM. THE TOP IS CREATED BY MAKING SIX TRIANGLES THAT MELD TOGETHER INTO A PINWHEEL SHAPE ON TOP OF THE HAT. IT'S AN EXCELLENT INTRODUCTION TO CIRCULAR KNITTING.

INSTRUCTIONS

Note: If you adapt other yarns and needle sizes to this pattern, you must try to get a base of about 18"/45.7cm circumference for an adult-size hat. Make sure to cast on stitches in multiples of 6 to top the hat with 6 triangles. This hat is worked in-the-round from the bottom up.

Cast on 84 stitches.

Place marker. Join and start knitting in-the-round, carefully making sure not to twist the cast-on row.

Step 1

Make Brim.

Round 1: K.

Round 2: P.

Continue in circular garter stitch until brim measures 5"/12.7cm or desired height.

Step 2

Make Crown.

Note: Instructions follow for 14 stitches in each of the 6 triangles. If you have adapted the pattern for a different size, adjust the pattern accordingly.

Upright Equilateral Triangle 1:

Row 1: K1inc1, turn, s1; turn—1 st left unknitted.

Row 2: K1inc1, k1, turn; pm1, s1, k1, turn—2 sts left unknitted.

Row 3: K1inc1, pm2, k to marker1, rm1, k1, turn; pm1, s1, k to marker2, rm2, k1, turn.

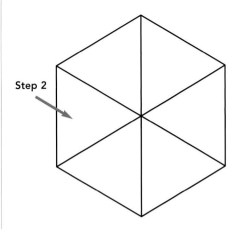

Step 2

Repeat row 3 until there are 13 sts left unknitted and remove all markers.

Last row: K1inc1, k13, *do not turn*.

Place the 13 sts that have been left unknitted and the 1st st of the k1inc1 in the last row on stitch holder 1. These will be used at the end of the project to attach the 6th triangle. Continue as follows:

Upright Equilateral Triangle 2:

Row 1: K1, turn; skp, turn.

Row 2: S1, k1, turn; pm1, s1, skp, turn.

Row 3: S1, pm2, k to marker1, rm1, k1, turn; pm1, s1, k to marker2, rm2, skp, turn.

Repeat row 3 until there are 14 sts.

End with: pm2, s1, k to marker1, rm1, k1.

Next row: S1, k12, skp, turn. Put last skp stitch on stitch holder 2 (these stitches will be used to complete the top ring of the hat).

Last row: K13, *do not turn*.

MATERIALS

Approx total: 100 yd/90 m worsted-weight yarn that knits up at 20 sts to 4"/10cm.

Knitting needles: 4.5mm (size 7 U.S.) 16"/41cm circular needles *or size to obtain gauge*

Extra needle for three-needle bind-off

2 stitch holders

2 stitch markers

Tapestry needle

FINISHED MEASUREMENTS

Approx 21"/53.3cm circumference x 4"/10cm height

GAUGE

16 sts and 32 rows = 4"/10cm in Circular Garter Stitch

Always take time to check your gauge.

PATTERN STITCHES

UPRIGHT TRIANGLES
See page 29, and make a small practice swatch if you have never used this technique before.

CIRCULAR GARTER STITCH
Round 1: Knit.

Round 2: Purl.

Repeat rounds 1 and 2 for pattern.

Triangles 3 to 6:

Work rows 1 to 3 of Triangle 2 once, then continue to repeat row 3 until 12 sts rem.

Next row: S1, k12, turn.
Next row: S1, k11, skp. Put 1 stitch left from previous Triangle on stitch holder 2 (increase number of stitches on holder by 1 each for each triangle—3, 4, 5, 6 stitches).
Last row: K13, *do not turn.*

FINISHING

Turn the hat inside out. Join the 14 sts on stitch holder 1 with the 14 stitches just knitted using the three-needle bind-off.

Cut yarn, leaving approximately a 5"/12.7cm tail.

Take the 5 sts off stitch holder 2. Thread tapestry needle onto

5"/12.7cm tail, and pull yarn through all these stitches. Refer to the Closing Holes technique (see page 15) to close the space between holes as you tighten the top of the hat. Pull tightly, knot and weave in any ends.

THIS HAT WAS KNIT WITH:

1 BALL NORO'S SILK GARDEN, 45% SILK/45% KID MOHAIR/10% WOOL, 1.6OZ/50G = 110YD/100M PER BALL, COLOR #88

ZIGZAG SCARF

WITH JUST ONE BASIC SHAPE, THIS SCARF IS AN EXCELLENT INTRODUCTION TO DIAGONAL KNITTING. THE BRIGHT RAYON YARN ACCENTUATES THE PATTERN WITH ITS INTERESTING COLOR CHANGES, GLOSSY SHINE, AND LUXURIOUS DRAPE. EXPERIMENT WITH DIFFERENT YARNS TO SEE HOW THE TEXTURE CHANGES WITH EACH FIBER. USE WOOL FOR WINTER, AND COTTON FOR SUMMER.

MATERIALS

Approx total: 345 yd/316m light worsted-weight yarn that knits up at 20 sts to 4"/10cm

Knitting needles: 4.5mm (size 7 U.S.) *or size to obtain gauge*

Stitch marker

FINISHED MEASUREMENTS

Approx 4"/10cm wide x 60"/152.4cm long

GAUGE

18 sts and 36 rows = 4"/10cm in Garter Stitch

Always take time to check your gauge.

PATTERN STITCHES

DIAGONAL TRIANGLES
See page 28, and make a small practice swatch if you have never used this technique before.

Note: Triangles are knit at the base of the scarf. They disappear as you work the diagonal zigzag rows.

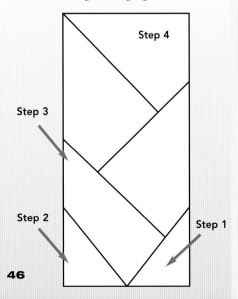

INSTRUCTIONS

Step 1

Make a Right Triangle.

Using knitted cast-on method, CO 9 sts.

Row 1: K1inc1, k1, turn; pm, s1, k to end, turn.

Row 2: K1inc1, k to marker, rm, k1, turn; pm, s1, k to end, turn.

Repeat row 2 until all 9 CO sts have been used up, ending with: k1inc1, k to marker, rm, k1, *do not turn*—17 sts.

Step 2

Make another Right Triangle.

Without cutting the yarn, repeat instructions to make another Right Triangle that will result in a facing Base Triangle on the other side.

Next row: S1, pm, k to end, turn.

Step 3

Work zigzag shapes.

Row 1: K1inc1, k to marker, rm, skp, turn; s1, pm, k to end, turn.

Repeat row 1 until there are 9 sts left, ending with k1inc1, k to marker, rm, skp, pm, *do not turn*, k9, turn. (Make sure to place the marker back after you have completed the skp.)

Repeat these instructions again facing the opposite direction, and continue repeating instructions, switching directions with each repetition until scarf is desired length.

Step 4

End scarf with Ending Triangle.

Row 1: K1inc1, k to marker, rm, skp, turn; s1, pm, k to end, turn.

Repeat row 1 until there are 17 unknitted sts left (17 knitted sts), ending with k1inc1, k to marker, rm, skp, turn; s1, pm, k to last 1 st—1 st left unknitted on the right needle.

Next row: S1, pass 2nd st on right needle over 1st st, k to marker, rm, skp, turn; s1, pm, k to last 1 st, turn—1 st left unknitted on the right needle.

Repeat this row until there are 3 sts left of Ending Triangle.

FINISHING

BO all sts, weave in ends.

THIS SCARF WAS KNIT WITH:

1 SKEIN OF BLUE HERON'S BEADED RAYON, 100% RAYON, APPROX 8OZ/226G = 525 YDS/ 480M PER SKEIN, COLOR DAFFODIL

SHAPES

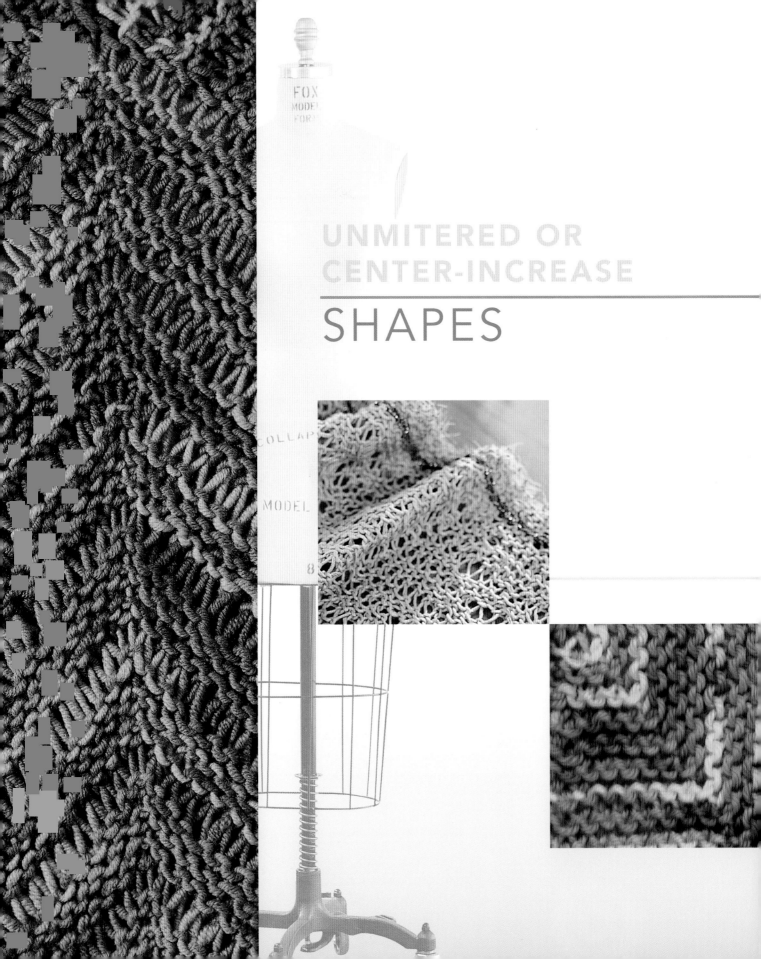

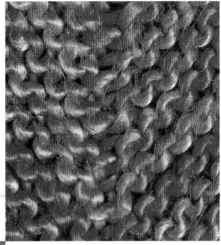

I N THIS CHAPTER, YOU WILL LEARN TO KNIT SYMMETRICAL CENTER-INCREASE SHAPES IN A CONTINUOUS WAY. YOU WILL ALSO LEARN HOW THIS STITCH DIFFERS FROM THE CENTER-DECREASE SHAPES.

SHAPES TO LEARN

There are many reasons for choosing the center-increase or unmitered square or triangle over the center-decrease or mitered square or triangle (see page 82). There is one major difference between the two techniques:

■ In the center-increase shapes, the number of stitches on the needles keeps increasing, and all stitches remain on the needles when the shape is complete.

■ In the center-decrease shapes (sometimes called "dominos") typically used for modular knitting, all stitches are bound off, and in order to continue adding more modules, you must pick up new stitches.

If you are working on a large project such as a blanket or afghan, where the knitted work will become too heavy or there will be too many stitches on the needle for you to handle, you may find the mitered center-decrease method easier to manage. In addition, if your project requires frequent yarn changes and you will need to cut the yarn and weave in ends anyway, then the traditional mitered method is best. However, if you are developing a project with one or two yarns and dislike the effort of binding off and picking up stitches, then this method is for you.

SHAPES TO LEARN

1 CENTER-INCREASE TRIANGLES (FIGURE 1)

2 CENTER-INCREASE SQUARE OR DIAMOND (FIGURE 2)

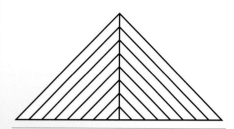

Figure 1

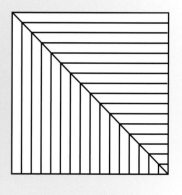

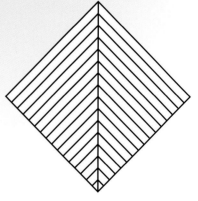

Figure 2

CENTER-INCREASE TRIANGLE

In this exercise, you will make a 13 x 13 x 13 stitch triangle.

Step 1

Begin the triangle.

Using knitted cast on, CO 13 sts. Turn and k13.

Step 2

Make the triangle.

Row 1: K6, k1inc1, k1, turn; s1, k1inc1, k2, turn—5 sts.

Note: When you turn in the middle of a row, this creates a gap. The stitches counted for the triangle are those between the gaps.

Row 2: S1, k1, k1inc1, k3, turn; s1, k2, k1inc1, k4, turn—9 sts.

Row 3: S1, k3, k1inc1, k5, turn; s1, k4, k1inc1, k6—13 sts.

Row 4: S1, k5, k1inc1, k7, turn; s1, k6, k1inc1, k8—17 sts.

Row 5: S1, k7, k1inc1, k9, turn; s1, k8, k1inc1, k10—21 sts.

Row 6: S1, k9, k1inc1, k11, turn; s1, k10, k1inc1, k12—25 sts.

Row 7: S1, k11, k1inc1, k12—26 sts.

Repeat Steps 1 and 2 to add additional triangles.

Bind off when complete.

CENTER-INCREASE SQUARE OR DIAMOND

Note: A tilted center-increase square is actually a diamond, and this shape is used in many of the projects in this book.

In this exercise, you will knit a Center-Increase Square that is 5 x 5 stitches.

Step 1

Begin the Square.

Cast on 5 stitches using any cast-on method you wish.

Step 2

Knit the Square.

Using the knitted cast on, CO 5 more sts—10 sts.

Row 1: K4, k1inc1, skp, turn.

Row 2: S1, k1inc1, k1, skp, turn—5 sts.

Row 3: S1, k1, k1inc1, k1, skp, turn—6 sts.

Row 4: S1, k1, k1inc1, k2, skp, turn—7 sts.

Row 5: S1, k2, k1inc1, k2, skp, turn—8 sts.

Row 6: S1, k2, k1inc1, k3, skp, turn—9 sts.

Row 7: S1, k3, k1inc1, k3, skp, turn—10 sts.

Note: To knit several squares side by side, repeat Step 1 but cast on in multiples of 5 to accommodate the number of squares you'd like. Then work Step 2 once to knit the first square.

For the subsequent squares:

Row 8: K2, turn.

Rows 9 to 14: Repeat rows 2 to 7 of Step 2.

Repeat Rows 8 to 14 until you have completed the number of side-by-side squares you would like.

Bind off.

USING MARKERS TO KEEP YOUR PLACE

In the patterns that follow, one marker is used to identify the center stitch on each row where the K1inc1 increase stitch takes place. Note that once you have started your diamond, you will be able to identify that stitch without a marker—it is the 2nd stitch of the K1inc1 from the previous row, a stitch that has a bar under it and appears as a "half" stitch. You will use additional markers to mark the end of each row that is attached to the adjoining diamond with a skp. Once again, there is a clear way to identify the stitch at the end of each row—there is always a gap between that stitch and the stitches from the adjoining diamond. Once you recognize the gap, you will knit to the stitch before the gap, then skp to close the gap with the stitch following the gap. Learn to identify these stitches, so that markers will no longer be necessary.

ELEGANT TABLE RUNNER

NEED TO QUICKLY SPRUCE UP YOUR TABLE FOR A DINNER PARTY? THIS RUNNER, EASY ENOUGH TO WHIP UP DURING A COUPLE OF NIGHTS WATCHING TV, COMBINES DROP-STITCH GARTER LACE WITH UNMITERED TRIANGLES FOR TRIM. METALLIC YARN TASSELS ON THE ENDS ADD A GLIMMER OF GLAMOUR. IF YOU'RE FEELING WHIMSICAL, WEAR IT AS A SCARF!

MATERIALS

Yarn A: 226yd/206.6m of DK-weight cotton yarn that knits up at 22 sts to 4"/10cm

Yarn B: 10yd/9.1m of novelty yarn for edging trim

Yarn C: 20yd/18.3m of metallic yarn for crochet trim

Knitting needles: 4.5mm (size 7 U.S.) straight and 4.5mm (size 7 U.S.) 29"/74cm circular needles *or size to obtain gauge*

Crochet hook: 4.5mm (size H U.S.)

FINISHED MEASUREMENTS

Approx 53"/134.6cm long x 8"/20.3cm wide without fringe

GAUGE

12 sts x 42 rows = 4"/10 cm in Drop-stitch Garter

Always take time to check your gauge.

PATTERN STITCHES

CENTER-INCREASE TRIANGLES
See page 51, and make a small practice swatch if you have never used this technique before.

DROP-STITCH GARTER
Work a yo between each stitch.

On the next row, drop the yarn overs to create elongated stitches.

INSTRUCTIONS

Step 1

Make Runner Body Rectangle.

With A, cast on 145 sts.

Rows 1 to 5: K.

Row 6: K1, *yo, k1; repeat from * to end.

Row 7: K1, *dyo, k1; repeat from * to end.

Rows 8 to 14: K.

Rows 15 and 16: Repeat rows 6 and 7.

Repeat rows 8 to 16 seven more times.

Last 5 rows: K.

Bind off all sts loosely.

Step 2

Make Center-Increase Triangles on ends.

With A, pick up 27 stitches evenly across one end.

Cut yarn. Slip 13 sts to the other needle.

Row 1: K1inc1, k1, turn; s1, k1inc1, k2, turn.

Row 2: S1, k1, k1inc1, k3, turn; s1, k2, k1inc1, k4, turn—9 sts worked in triangle.

Row 3: S1, k3, k1inc1, k5, turn; s1, k4, k1inc1, k6, turn—13 sts.

Row 4: S1 (yo, k1) 5 times, k1inc1, (yo, k1) 7 times, turn; dropping all YO's when you come to them, s1 k6, k1inc1, k8, turn.

Row 5: S1, k7, k1inc1, k9, turn; s1, k8, k1inc1, k10, turn—21 sts.

Row 6: S1, k9, k1inc1, k11, turn; s1, k10, k1inc1, k12, turn—25 sts.

Row 7: S1 (yo, k1) 11 times, k1inc1, (yo, k1) 13 times, turn; dropping all YO's when you come to them, s1 k12, k1inc1, k14, turn.

Row 8: S1, k13, k1inc1, k15, turn; s1, k14, k1inc1, k16, turn—33 sts.

Row 9: S1, k15, k1inc1, k17, turn; s1, k16, k1inc1, k18, turn—37 sts.

Row 10: S1, k17, k1inc1, k19, turn; s1, k18, k1inc1, k20, turn—41 sts.

Row 11: S1 (yo, k1) 19 times, k1inc1, (yo, k1) 21 times, turn; dropping all YO's when you come to them, s1 k20, k1inc1, k22, turn.

Row 12: S1, k21, k1inc1, k23, turn; s1, k22, k1inc1, k24, turn—49 sts.

Row 13: S1, k23, k1inc1, k25, turn; s1, k24, k1inc1, k26, turn—53 sts.

Row 14: S1, k25, k1inc1, k26—54 sts.

Bind off all sts. Cut yarn.

Repeat Step 2 on other side of Runner Body.

FINISHING

Crochet Trim

With crochet hook, attach B (novelty yarn) and work 1 row of single crochet around outside edge of entire runner.

Metallic Trim

With crochet hook, attach C (metallic yarn) and work 1 row of single crochet onto long stitches created by dropped yarn overs on the surface of the Triangles. In addition, single crochet into the first and last set of long stitches created in the Runner Body Rectangle.

Fringe

Cut six 16"/40.6cm lengths of novelty yarn (B) and five 16"/40.6cm lengths of metallic yarn (C) for each fringe. Create fringe as follows:

Holding 6 strands of B and 5 strands of C together evenly, fold them in half to make a loop. Insert the crochet hook into a stitch at the point on one end of the runner. Catch all the strands in the center and draw the loop end through, making it large enough so you can pull the ends of the yarn through the loop. Pull down on the ends so that the loops tighten snugly around the stitch.

Repeat on the other end of the runner.

THIS RUNNER WAS KNIT WITH:

(A) 2 BALLS OF BOUTON D'OR'S ALEXANDRIE, 100% COTTON, 1.8OZ/50G = 113YD/104M, COLOR 431 GREEN

(B) 1 BALL OF HABU TEXTILES A28 KASUMI, 100% POLYESTER, .5OZ/14G= 121YD/109M, COLOR KASU (NOVELTY YARN)

(C) 1 BALL OF IRONSTONE YARNS' PARIS NIGHTS, 67% ACRYLIC/12% METAL/21% NYLON, APPROX 1.8OZ/50G = 205YD/187M, COLOR 13 ALBAN (METALLIC YARN)

MATERIALS

Approx. total:

Yarn A: 200yd/183m (baby 6 months) to 1000yd/914m (extra-large adult) worsted-weight yarn that knits up at 20 sts to 4"/10cm

Yarn B: 20yd/18m of ¼"/6mm ribbon yarn for trim

Knitting needles: 5.5mm (size 9 U.S.) *or size to obtain gauge*

3 stitch markers

Stitch holder

Tapestry needle

Washable fabric glue

Extra needle for three-needle bind-off

FINISHED MEASUREMENTS

This poncho can be made to any size. Instructions are given for baby 6-month and women's medium, with notes on adapting the pattern to any other size.

Baby 6-month, 9"/22.9cm: Diamond measured from top to bottom on diagonal

Women's medium, 19"/48.3cm: Diamond measured from top to bottom on diagonal

GAUGE

13 sts and 26 rows = 4"/10cm x 4"/10cm diamond in Center-Increase Squares Pattern Stitch

Always take time to check your gauge.

(Pattern stitches are listed on page 58.)

LACE RIBBON PONCHO

THIS PONCHO CAN BE MADE IN ANY SIZE, FOR EVERY MEMBER OF YOUR FAMILY. JUST MAKE THE FIRST DIAMOND LONG ENOUGH TO REACH FROM THE WEARER'S NECK TO THEIR WAIST, AND THE PONCHO WILL BE LONG ENOUGH. THIS IS A VARIATION OF THE CENTER-INCREASE SQUARE; THE KNITTED CAST ON IS NOT USED, BUT INSTEAD THE STITCHES ARE ADDED ON A ROW-BY-ROW BASIS. THIS UNIQUE METHOD OF ADDING STITCHES RESULTS IN A NICE EDGE, AND GIVES YOU THE OPPORTUNITY TO KEEP INCREASING THE FIRST SQUARE TO THE SIZE YOU WANT, INSTEAD OF PREDETERMINING ITS SIZE.

3-needle bind-off

PATTERN STITCHES

CENTER-INCREASE SQUARES

See page 51, and make a small practice swatch if you have never used this technique before.

DOUBLE-YO OPENWORK

Work a double yo between each knit stitch as indicated in pattern.

On the next row, drop the yarn overs to create elongated stitches.

INSTRUCTIONS

Cast on 2 stitches.

Step 1

Make Diamond 1.

Row 1: K1inc1, k1—3 sts.

Row 2: K1inc1, k1inc1, k1—5 sts.

Row 3: K1inc1, k1inc1, pm, k2, p1—7 sts.

Row 4: S1, k to marker, rm, k1inc1, pm, k to last st, p1—8 sts.

Row 5: Add a yo between every stitch in this row as follows: S1, ★yo, k1; rep from ★ to marker, rm, yo, k1inc1, pm ★yo, k1, rep to last 1 st, p1.

Row 6: Drop all yo stitches in this row: S1, k to marker, rm, k1inc1, pm, k1, k to last 1 st, p1—10 sts.

Rows 7 and 8: S1, k to marker, rm, k1inc1, pm, k to last 1 st, p1—12 sts after row 8 is worked.

Row 9: Add a double yo between every stitch in this row as follows: S1, ★double yo, k1; rep from ★ to marker, rm, double yo, k1inc1, pm ★double yo, k1, rep to last 1 st, p1.

Row 10: Drop all yo stitches in this row: S1, k to marker, rm, k1inc1, pm, k1, k to last 1 st, p1—14 sts.

Rows 11 and 12: S1, k to marker, rm, k1inc1, pm, k to last 1 st, p1—16 sts after row 12 is worked.

Rep rows 5 to 12 until the height of diamond measures the length you want the poncho to be. The Diamond should cover the entire back and should extend from the neck down as far as you'd like the poncho to reach.

Last row: S1, k to marker, rm, k1inc1, pm, k to end.

Place the stitches on the right side of Diamond 1, including the first stitch of the k1inc1 in the center, on a stitch holder. Those stitches will be attached later to close the poncho.

Step 2

Make Diamond 2.

Note: You'll be using 2 markers in this Diamond and all subsequent ones: one to mark the position of the k1inc1 in the center, and one to mark the place where you will need to skp to attach the new diamond to the previous diamond.

Following the order in the diagram on page 58, end at one of the corners of Diamond 1 and begin Diamond 2 as follows:

Row 1: K1inc1, turn; s1, k1, turn—2 sts.

Row 2: K1inc1, skp, turn; s1, k1inc1, pl—4 sts.

Row 3: S1, k1inc1, k1, skp, turn—5 sts.

Row 4: S1, pm, k1, k1inc1, pm, k1, p1.

Row 5: S1, k to marker, rm, k1inc1, pm, k to marker, rm, skp, turn.

Row 6: S1, pm, k to marker, rm, k1inc1, pm, k to last 1 st, p1, turn.

Row 7: Add a yo between every stitch in this row as follows: S1, ★yo, k1; rep from ★ to marker, rm, yo, k1inc1, pm, ★yo, k1, rep to marker, rm, yo, skp, turn.

Row 8: Drop all yo stitches in this row as follows: S1, pm, k to marker, rm, k1inc1, pm, k to last 1 st, p1, turn.

Row 9: S1, k to marker, rm, k1inc1, pm, k to marker, rm, skp, turn.

Row 10: S1, pm, k to marker, rm, k1inc1, pm, k to last 1 st, p1, turn.

Row 11: Add a double yo between every stitch in this row as follows: S1, ★double yo, k1; rep from ★ to marker, rm, double yo, k1inc1, pm, ★double yo, k1, rep to marker, rm, double yo, skp, turn.

Row 12: Drop all double yo stitches in this row: S1, pm, k to marker, rm, k1inc1, pm, k to last 1 st, p1, turn.

Rows 13 and 14: Repeat rows 9 and 10.

Rep rows 7 to 14, ending with row 13 when you have connected a skp to the last stitch that remains of previously knitted Diamond 1 that is not on the stitch holder (this is the center stitch, the 2nd stitch of the k1inc1 on the previous row).

Turn and work the last row of Diamond 2 as follows:

Last row: Bind off all stitches to marker, rm, k1inc1, pm, k to last 1 st, s1.

Step 3
Make Diamond 3.

Repeat the instructions for Diamond 2 to create this 3rd Diamond. However, when you have connected with the skp the last stitch of previously knitted Diamond 2, work the last rows as follows:

Row 1: S1, pm, k to marker, rm, k1inc1, pm, k to last 1 st, s1, turn.

Row 2: Bind off all stitches to marker, rm, k1inc1, pm, k to marker, rm, skp, turn.

Step 4
Make Diamond 4.

Repeat the instructions for Diamond 2 to create this 4th Diamond. However, when you have connected with the skp the last stitch of previously knitted Diamond 3, work the last rows as follows:

Row 1: Bind off all stitches to marker, rm, k1inc1, pm, k to end.

FINISHING

Connect the side of Diamond 1 with the side of Diamond 4 using a three-needle bind-off. Cut yarn, and weave in ends.

Decorate with Ribbon

Starting with the bottom of Diamond 1, weave the ribbon through the 1st, 4th, 6th, 7th, and 8th double yo rows as follows:

Cut a 30"/76.2cm length of the ribbon yarn, and thread through a large tapestry needle. Weave the ribbon in and out of the large stitches made by the double yo's. When you have completed a row, cut the ribbon. Adhere each ribbon end to an adjacent exposed bit of ribbon on the wrong side using washable fabric glue. Repeat the process following the pattern above for each of the additional three Diamonds.

THIS PONCHO WAS KNIT WITH:

(A) 5 skeins of ARTYARNS SUPERMERINO, 100% MERINO WOOL, 1.8OZ/50G = 104YD/95M PER SKEIN, IN COLOR #115 REDS

(B) 1 SKEIN GREAT ADIRONDACK'S IRISEE RIBBON, 95% RAYON/5% POLYESTER, 100YD/91M PER SKEIN, COLOR MANGO

BUILDING
BLOCKS
SHAWL

F YOU HAVE NEVER KNIT UNMITERED SQUARES BEFORE, THIS PROJECT IS FOR YOU. ALTHOUGH IT LOOKS COMPLICATED WITH TWO COLORS, YOU CHANGE YARN AFTER EVERY TWO ROWS, AND YOU DON'T CUT THE YARN, SO THERE ARE NO EXTRA ENDS TO WEAVE IN. WITH JUST TWO STRIPS OF SQUARES THAT ARE SEWN TOGETHER AFTER YOU FINISH KNITTING, YOU CAN MAKE THIS OVER THE WEEKEND TO SPRUCE UP YOUR MONDAY WARDROBE.

INSTRUCTIONS

Note: Throughout you will be alternating Colors A and B, knitting 2 rows of each, one on the right side, and one on the reverse. Do not cut any of the yarns—just start knitting with each color, making sure you are carrying the yarn up the wrong side so it does not show on the right side. You knit two separate strips, and sew them together after you finish knitting.

Step 1

Work first strip of Center-Increase Squares.

With A, cast on 20 stitches. Using the knitted cast on, CO an additional 20 stitches.

Begin Square 1.

Row 1: With A, k22, turn.

Row 2 (RS): With A, s1, k1inc1, skp, turn.

Row 3 (WS): With A, s1, pm1, k1inc1, pm2, k1, skp, turn.

Row 4 (RS): Attach B. Do not cut A.

With B, s1, pm3, k to marker 2, rm2, k1inc1, pm2, k to marker 1, rm1, skp, turn.

Row 5 (WS): With B, s1, pm1, k to marker 2, rm2, k1inc1, pm2, k to marker 3, rm3, skp, turn.

Repeat rows 4 and 5 with A, and then B, alternating colors until square is 39 sts. End as follows:

Next row: With A, s1, k18, k1inc1, k19, turn; k to end.

Next row: With A and B together, bind off 20 sts, k to end—total 20 sts left.

Work Squares 2 to 6.

With A, cast on 20 stitches using the knitted cast on.

Repeat instructions for Square 1, alternating colors every 2 rows.

Continue adding squares until you have completed 9 squares. Add additional squares if you want a longer scarf. With A, bind off all sts.

MATERIALS

Approx total: 600yd/548.6m worsted-weight yarn that knits up at 20 sts to 4"/10cm.

Color A: 300yd/274.3m solid

Color B: 300yd/274.3m variegated

Knitting needles: 4.5mm (size 7 U.S.) *or size to obtain gauge*

Crochet hook: 10mm (size N U.S.)

Tapestry needle for sewing strips

3 stitch markers

FINISHED MEASUREMENTS

Approx 60"/152.4cm long x 9"/22.9cm wide

GAUGE

18 sts x 34 rows = 4"/10cm in Garter Stitch

Always take time to check your gauge.

PATTERN STITCHES

CENTER-INCREASE SQUARES
See page 51, and make a small practice swatch if you have never used this technique before.

Note: Because of the color changes, the pattern does not follow the exercise exactly, although it is similar enough that it will be helpful to practice it prior to starting this project.

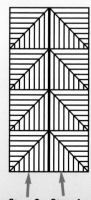

Step 2   Step 1

Step 2

Work second Strip of Center-Increase Squares—Mirror-Image Squares Strip.

With A, cast on 20 stitches. K to end. Cast on 20 additional stitches using the knitted cast on.

Repeat instructions for Square 1 above, *but switch colors on the odd-numbered rows (now these are RS rows),* **not** *on the even-numbered rows (now these are WS rows).*

Continue until Strip 2 has the same number of squares as Strip 1.

Step 3

Work end of scarf.

After you have completed row 40 of the last square, cast off all stitches with A. Cut yarn. Weave in ends.

FINISHING

Sew the two strips together, with WS facing. Using a cool iron, press gently to flatten shawl.

THIS SHAWL WAS KNIT WITH:

6 SKEINS OF ARTYARNS SUPERMERINO, 100% MERINO WOOL, APPROX 1.8OZ/50G = 104YD/95M PER SKEIN

(A) 3 SKEINS COLOR #107 BLUE

(B) 3 SKEINS COLOR #103 YELLOW

CHEVRON TIE

EVER WISH YOUR HUSBAND OR BOYFRIEND WOULD WEAR SOMETHING YOU'VE KNITTED FOR HIM? THIS UNDERSTATED TIE IS THE PERFECT SOLUTION. YOU CAN MAKE IT IN A WEEKEND AS A SURPRISE GIFT FOR THAT SPECIAL GUY IN YOUR LIFE. (IT LOOKS GREAT ON GIRLS, TOO!)

MATERIALS

Approx total: 163yd/274.3m DK-weight silk yarn that knits up at 20 sts to 4"/10cm

Knitting needles: 3.25mm (Size 3 U.S.) *or size to obtain gauge*

Crochet hook: 1.6mm (size 6 U.S.) steel hook

Tapestry needle

FINISHED MEASUREMENTS

Approx 1 3/4"/4.4cm wide x 62"/157.5cm long

GAUGE

20 sts x 40 rows = 4"/10cm in Garter Stitch

Always take time to check your gauge.

PATTERN STITCHES

CENTER-INCREASE EQUILATERAL TRIANGLE
See page 51, and make a small practice swatch if you have never used this technique before.

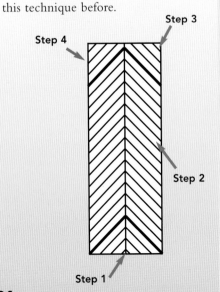

Step 4
Step 3
Step 2
Step 1

INSTRUCTIONS

Cast on 9 stitches.

Step 1

Make Bottom Triangle.

Row 1: K4, k1inc1, k1, turn; s1, k1inc1, k2, turn—5 sts.

Note: When you turn in the middle of a row, this creates a gap. The stitches counted for the triangle are those between the gaps.

Row 2: S1, k1, k1inc1, k3, turn; s1, k2, k1inc1, k4, turn—9 sts.

Row 3: S1, k3, k1inc1, k5, turn; s1, k4, k1inc1, k6, turn—13 sts.

Row 4: S1, k5, k1inc1, k7, turn; s1, k6, k1inc1, k8—17 sts.

Step 2

Make the Tie Body, working across all sts.

Row 1: K2tog, k6, k1inc1, k8—17 sts.

Repeat row 1 until tie measures 12"/30.5cm.

Decrease the width of the tie as follows:

Row 1: K2tog, k2tog, k4, k1inc1, k8—16 sts.

Row 2: K2tog, k2tog, k4, k1inc1, k7—15sts.

Row 3: K2tog, k5, k1inc1,k7—15 sts.

Repeat row 3 until tie measures 20"/50.8cm.

Continue to decrease the width of the tie as follows:

Row 1: K2tog, k2tog, k3, k1inc1, k7—14 sts.

Row 2: K2tog, k2tog, k3, k1inc1, k6—13sts.

Row 3: K2tog, k4, k1inc1, k6—13 sts.

Repeat row 3 until tie measures 67"/170.1cm.

Step 3

Make Tie Ending Triangle Right Side.

Row 1: K2tog, k4, s1, turn; s2, pass first slipped st over second slipped st, k4, turn.

Row 2: K2tog, k2, s1, turn; s2, pass first slipped st over second slipped st, k2, turn.

Row 3: k2tog, s1, turn; s2, pass first slipped st over second slipped st.

Cut yarn and pull through last loop to fasten.

Step 4

Make Tie Ending Triangle Left Side.

Slide all stitches over on needle so that opposite side is ready to be worked.

Attach yarn to this end of work.

Note: Because the opposite side is being worked at this point, you will be using reverse garter stitch (p on every row) to maintain uniformity.

Row 1: P2tog, p3, s1, turn; s2, pass first slipped st over second slipped st, p3, turn.

Row 2: P2tog, p1, s1, turn; s2, pass first slipped st over second slipped st, p1, turn.

Row 3: P2tog.

Cut yarn and pull through last loop to fasten.

FINISHING

Cut yarn, weave in ends.

Make tie loop (for keeping tie flat):

Insert crochet hook into side approximately 9"/22.9cm up from tie end into the right side. Pull loop, and chain 11. Single crochet into left edge directly opposite to attach loop. Cut yarn, weave in ends.

THESE TIES WERE KNIT WITH:

1 SKEIN ARTYARNS ROYAL SILK, 100% SILK, APPROX 1.8OZ/50G = 163 YDS/149M PER SKEIN, COLOR #110 PINK AND COLOR #123 GREENS AND BLUES

NOTE: THIS TIE CAN BE MADE WITH VARIOUS YARN WEIGHTS.

OTHER

SHORT ROW SHA

S

IN THIS CHAPTER, YOU WILL LEARN NEW MULTIDIRECTIONAL TECHNIQUES TO CREATE ADDITIONAL SHAPES THAT YOU CAN COMBINE WITH THE BASIC SHAPES YOU HAVE ALREADY LEARNED. YOU ARE ON YOUR WAY TO NEW HEIGHTS OF CREATIVITY!

SHAPES TO LEARN

1 BULL'S-EYE SQUARE

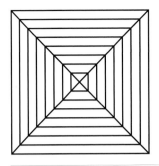

Figure 1

2 CUT-OUT KNITTING

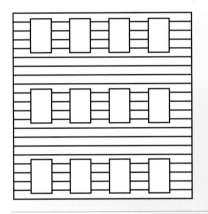

Figure 2

BULL'S-EYE SQUARE

In this exercise, you will learn how to make a square that has a symmetrically knitted center. This effect is particularly noticeable with variegated yarn, where the color clusters are not in the corner of a square, but smack in the middle.

Cast on 20 sts.

Step 1

Make first half of Square (Triangle with center decrease).

Row 1: K9, k2tog, k9.

Row 2: S1, k8, k2tog, k7, turn—1 st on right side left unknitted.

Row 3: S1, k6, k2tog, k7, turn—1 st on left side left unknitted.

Row 4: S1, k6, k2tog, k5, turn—2 sts on right side left unknitted.

Row 5: S1, k4, k2tog, k5, turn—2 sts on left side left unknitted.

Row 6: S1, k4, k2tog, k3, turn—3 sts on right side left unknitted.

Row 7: S1, k2, k2tog, k3, turn—3 sts on left side left unknitted.

Row 8: S1, k2, k2tog, k1, turn—4 sts on right side left unknitted.

Row 9: S1, k2tog, k1, turn—4 sts on left side left unknitted.

You should now have a total of 11 sts on the needles, including 4 from the right side and 4 from the left side.

At this point, most of the sts on the needle appear widely spaced apart. If you ignore that and knit with them the way they are, you will find holes in your work. To prevent holes, make 1 (m1) every time you pick up a new stitch from the previous triangle as follows:

1. Make an extra stitch by inserting right needle into the front of top vertical stitch from the previous row to pick it up (you will find this stitch positioned halfway between the first stitch on the right needle and the first stitch on the left needle).

2. Place the stitch on the left needle so it is in a position to be knitted.

3. Knit the newly made stitch and the next stitch together, to maintain the normal stitch count, but at the same time to ensure that there are no holes.

This is abbreviated m1k1.

Step 2

Make second half of Square (Triangle with center increase).

Row 10: S1, k1inc1, k1, m1k1, turn.

Row 11: S1, k1, k1inc1, k2, m1k1, turn.

Row 12: S1, k2, k1inc1, k3, m1k1, turn.

Row 13: S1, k3, k1inc1, k4, m1k1, turn.

Row 14: S1, k4, k1inc1, k5, m1k1, turn.

Row 15: S1, k5, k1inc1, k6, m1k1, turn.

Row 16: S1, k6, k1inc1, k7, m1k1, turn.

Row 17: S1, k7, k1inc1, k8, m1k1, turn.

Row 18: S1, k8, k1inc1, k9, m1k1, turn.

CUT-OUT KNITTING

In this exercise you will learn a style of knitting that uses spaces between groups of knitted stitches for dramatic effects. This flexible design feature does not have the limitations of traditional lace knitting and unraveling techniques to achieve spacing in knitwear. This tutorial will teach you how to make a swatch that inserts holes into horizontal garter stitch knitting. In the projects, this technique is combined with other shapes. For example, the Holes Scarf on page 70 combines vertical squares with cut-out knitting, and the Square Holes Sweater on page 76 combines unmitered squares with cut-out knitting.

Each panel is made up of 5 horizontal squares with 1-stitch spaces between each square (total 4 spaces).

Cast on 19 stitches.

Step 1

Make Square 1.

Row 1: ★K3, turn; k1inc1, k2, turn; rep from ★ 2 more times—6 sts worked.

Row 2: K3, bind off next 3 stitches— 3 sts rem on right needle.

Row 3: Bind off next 1 stitch (for 1-stitch space left between each square).

Step 2

Make Squares 2 to 4.

Row 1: K2, turn; k1inc1, k2, turn; ★k3, turn; k1inc1, k2, turn; rep from ★ 1 more time—6 sts worked.

Row 2: K3, bind off next 3 stitches— 3 additional sts rem on right needle.

Row 3: Bind off next 1 stitch (for 1-stitch space left between each square).

Step 3

Make Square 5.

Row 1: Bind off 1 st, k2, turn; ★k3, turn; rep from ★ 5 more times—15 sts total on needle.

Step 4

Join the Squares together.

Row 1: K3, ★k1inc1, k2; rep from ★ to end—19 sts.

Rows 2 and 3: K across all sts.

Repeat Steps 1 to 4 until you have reached desired length.

Bind off.

HOLES SCARF

THIS UNUSUAL SCARF CAN BE WORN AS A KEYHOLE SCARF, WITH ONE END THREADED THROUGH THE HOLES OF THE OTHER END. MADE IN A LIGHT-WEIGHT RAYON, ALL-SEASON YARN, THIS SCARF LOOKS EQUALLY GOOD WITH A TAILORED SUIT OR A FLIRTY CAMISOLE. MAKE A SECOND SCARF IN WOOL FOR A WINTER WARM-UP.

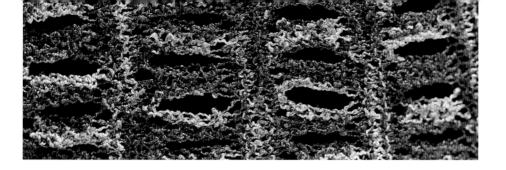

INSTRUCTIONS

Note: The original cast on used for this project is a long-tail cast on. Each hole panel (complete row of 4 holes) requires that 7 more stitches be added using the knitted cast on. This will keep the sides of the scarf consistent. An odd number of garter stitch rows separates the hole panels, so that the 7 stitches are added on alternate sides. This maintains the reversibility and symmetry of the scarf.

Cast on 19 sts.

Step 1

Make First Hole Panel.

Row 1: Using the knitted cast on, CO an additional 7 stitches and turn. K1inc1, k6, skp, turn.

Row 2: S1, k7, turn—1 st left unknitted.

Row 3: K1inc1, k6, skp, turn.

Row 4: S1, k7, turn—2 sts left unknitted.

Row 5: K1inc1, k1, then pass the stitch just increased over the k1 and off the needle as to bind off. Bind off the next 8 sts. Transfer last bound off st back to the left needle.

Repeat rows 1 to 5 three more times, and then repeat rows 1 to 4 once more.

Next row: K1inc1, k5, skp, turn; skp, and bind off next 6 sts—a total of 7 sts have been removed, leaving 2 sts on the left needle (in a separate little group) and 1 st on the right needle. ★K2, k1inc1; rep from ★ to last 2 sts, k2—19 sts.

Step 2

Work Garter Ridge between panels.

Rows 1 to 3: K.

Repeat Steps 1 and 2, ending with Step 1 when 13 panels are complete, or when scarf is desired length. Bind off all stitches.

FINISHING

Cut yarn, weave in ends.

THIS SCARF WAS KNIT WITH:

1 SKEIN OF FIESTA'S RAYON BOUCLE, 100% RAYON, 4OZ/112G = 220YDS/201M, COLOR SALSA

TIP: *If you've chosen a soft yarn for the project, you may choose to crochet a border around the scarf to add additional structure. Use a medium size crochet hook and single crochet around the entire scarf, making sure to single crochet 3 times into each of the 4 corners.*

MATERIALS

Approx total: 200yd/182.8m worsted-weight yarn that knits up at 20 sts to 4"/10cm

Knitting needles: 5mm (size 8 U.S.) *or size to obtain gauge*

FINISHED MEASUREMENTS

Approx 36"/91.4cm long x 4¾"/12cm wide

GAUGE

Single Hole Panel = 2"/5cm long x 4¾"/12cm wide

Always take time to check your gauge.

PATTERN STITCHES

CUT-OUT KNITTING

See page 69, and make a small practice swatch if you have never used this technique before.

GARTER STITCH

Knit every row.

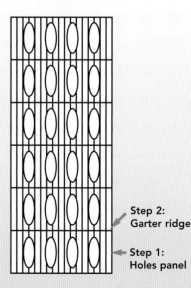

Step 2: Garter ridge

Step 1: Holes panel

BULL'S-EYE HAT

THE PATTERN STITCH IN THIS STRIKING HAT IS CHALLENGING AT FIRST, BUT YOU WILL QUICKLY WANT TO KNIT ANOTHER AS SOON AS YOU FINISH. BECAUSE THE HAT IS SO SMALL, IT IS A GOOD SUMMER KNITTING PROJECT TOO. EXPERIMENT WITH DIFFERENT PAIRS OF COLORS TO ACHIEVE A VARIETY OF LOOKS.

INSTRUCTIONS

With A, cast on 60 sts. Join and work Step 1 in the round.

Step 1

Make 5 Center-Increase Triangles.

Row 1: K5, k1inc1, k1, turn; s1, k1inc1, k1, turn.

Row 2: S1, k1inc1, k3, turn.

Row 3: Attach B, and with B, s1, k2, k1inc1, k3, turn—8 sts; s1, k2, k1inc1, k5, turn—10 sts.

Row 4: With A, s1, k4, k1inc1, k5, turn—12 sts; s1, k4, k1inc1, k7, turn—14 sts.

Row 5: With B, s1, k6, k1inc1, k7—16 sts, turn; s1, k6, k1inc1, k9, turn—18 sts.

Row 6: With A, s1, k8, k1inc1, k9—20 sts, turn; s1, k8, k1inc1, k11, turn—22 sts.

Row 7: with B, s1, k10, k1inc1, k11—24 sts, turn; S24, *do not turn.* Cut B.

Repeat rows 1 to 7 four more times to complete round and have a total of 5 triangles—120 sts.

With A, k12, turn (to the top of Triangle 1)—you are now in position to work Step 2.

Step 2

Make Bull's-Eye Diamonds.

First Half (Triangle with center decrease and live stitches remaining on top)

Row 1: With A, k11, skp, k11, turn.

Row 2: S1, k10, skp, k9, turn. Drop A, attach B.

Row 3: With B, s1, k8, skp, k9, turn.

Row 4: S1, k8, skp, k7, turn. Drop B, attach A.

Row 5: With A, s1, k6, skp, k7, turn.

Row 6: S1, k6, skp, k5, turn. Drop A, attach B.

Row 7: With B, s1, k4, skp, k5, turn.

Row 8: S1, k4, skp, k3, turn. Drop B, attach A.

Row 9: With A, s1, k2, skp, k3, turn.

Row 10: S1, k2, skp, k1, turn.

Row 11: S1, skp, k1, turn—13 sts.

Row 12: S1, k2, turn.

Second Half of Bull's-Eye Diamond (Triangle with center increase)

Row 1: With A, s1, k1inc1, k1, turn.

Row 2: S1, k1inc1, k3, turn. Drop A, attach B.

Row 3: With B, s1, k2, k1inc1, k3, turn.

Row 4: S1, k2, k1inc1, k5, turn. Drop B, attach A.

Row 5: With A, s1, k4, k1inc1, k5, turn.

Row 6: S1, k4, k1inc1, k7, turn. Drop A, attach B.

Row 7: With B, s1, k6, k1inc1, k7, turn.

Row 8: S1, k6, k1inc1, k9, turn. Cut B, attach A.

Row 9: With A, s1, k8, k1inc1, k9, turn.

MATERIALS

Approx total 120yd/109.7m worsted-weight wool or wool blend that knits up at approx 20 sts to 4"/10cm

Color A: 60yd/54.8m in black

Color B: 60yd/54.8m in white

Knitting needles: 5mm (size 8 U.S.) 16"/40cm circular needles *or size to obtain gauge*

2 stitch markers

2 stitch holders

Extra knitting needle for three-needle bind-off

FINISHED MEASUREMENTS

21"/53.3cm circumference x 4"/10cm height of brim

GAUGE

Single Triangle = 3"/7.6cm wide x 2"/5cm tall

Always take time to check your gauge.

PATTERN STITCHES

CENTER-INCREASE TRIANGLES
See page 51, and make a small practice swatch if you have never used this technique before.

BULL'S-EYE
See page 68, and make a small practice swatch if you have never used this technique before.

UPRIGHT EQUILATERAL TRIANGLES
See page 29, and make a small practice swatch if you have never used this technique before.

Step 4

Make Hat Top.

Equilateral Triangle 1:

Row 1: With A, k1inc1, turn.

Row 2: S1, turn—1 st left unknitted.

Row 3: K1inc1, k1, turn.

Row 4: Pm1, s1, k1, turn—2 sts left unknitted.

Row 5: K1inc1, pm2, k to marker1, rm1, k1, turn.

Row 6: S1, pm1, k to marker2, rm2, k1, turn (change the position of marker1 so it is after the first S1).

Repeat rows 5 and 6 until there are 10 sts left unknitted, and remove all markers. Drop A, attach B.

Last row: With B, k1inc1, k10, *do not turn.*

Place the 10 sts that have been left unknitted and the 1st st of the k1inc1 in the last row on stitch holder 1. These will be used at the end of the project to attach the 6th triangle.

Equilateral Triangle 2:

Row 1: With B, k1, turn.

Row 2: Skp. turn.

Row 3: S1, k1, turn.

Row 4: Pm1, s1, skp, turn.

Row 5: Pm2, s1, k to marker1, rm1, k1, turn.

Row 6: Pm1, s1, k to marker2, rm2, skp, turn.

Repeat rows 5 and 6 until 11 sts rem.

Next row: S1, k9, skp, turn. Put last skp stitch on stitch holder 2 (these

Row 10: S1, k8, k1inc1, k11, turn.

Row 11: S1, k10, k1inc1, k11, *do not turn.*

Repeat first and second halves of Bull's-Eye Diamonds 4 more times to make 5 diamonds. With A, k12 (to position yarn at the top of the Triangle before starting Step 3).

Step 3

Make Center-Decrease Triangles.

Repeat rows 1 to 11 of the first half of Bull's-Eye Diamond in Step 2, modifying row 11 so that you *do not turn*—S1, skp, k6, *do not turn,* 5 times to make 5 Center-Decrease Triangles—65 sts.

Round 1: With A, k1inc1, k to end of round—66 sts.

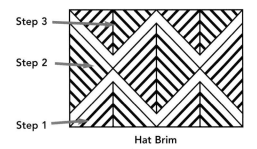

Hat Brim

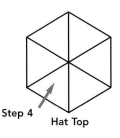

Hat Top

Other Short Row Shapes

Next row: S1, k9, skp, turn. Put last skp stitch on stitch holder 2 (these stitches will be used to complete the top ring of the hat). Drop B, attach A.

Last row: With A, k10, *do not turn*.

Triangles 3 to 6:

With A, work rows 1 to 6 once and then repeat rows 5 and 6 from Triangle 2 until you have 9 sts.

Next row: S1, k9, turn.
Next row: S1, k8, skp. Put 1 stitch left from previous Triangle on stitch holder 2 (increase number of stitches on holder by 1 each for each triangle—3, 4, 5 stitches). Drop A, attach B.
Last row: With B, k11, *do not turn*.

Work the remaining triangles in this way, alternating them in colors A and B, so that you have 3 triangles each in A and B.

FINISHING

Turn the hat inside out. Join the 11 stitches on stitch holder 1 with the 11 stitches just knitted as follows:

Move the stitches from stitch holder 1 to an extra needle facing them in the same direction as the stitches from Triangle 6. With A, use the three-needle bind-off to close the seam. (See page 17 for instructions on three-needle bind-off.)

Cut yarn, leaving approximately a 5"/12.7cm tail. Take the 5 stitches off stitch holder 2. Thread tapestry needle onto the 5"/12.7cm tail, and pull yarn through all these stitches. Refer to the Closing Holes technique (page 15) to close the space between holes as you tighten the top of the hat. Pull tightly, knot, and weave in any ends.

THIS HAT WAS KNIT WITH:

JAGGERSPUN'S ZEPHYR WOOL/SILK 4/8, 50% WOOL, 50% SILK, 4OZ/113G = 280YDS/256M

(A) 1 SKEIN COLOR BLACK

(B) 1 SKEIN COLOR WHITE

SQUARE HOLES SWEATER

T HE "UNMITERED" SQUARES THAT MAKE UP THE SWEATER ARE CONSTRUCTED IN THE OPPOSITE WAY OF TRADITIONAL MITERED SQUARES—THE SQUARES ARE INCREASED IN EVERY ROW INSTEAD OF DECREASED AND BOUND OFF. THIS LEAVES ALL THE STITCHES LIVE ON THE NEEDLES, AND NO PICKING UP OF STITCHES OR CUTTING OF YARN IS REQUIRED. THE HOLES OR CUT-OUTS ARE CREATED WITH A BIND OFF FOLLOWED BY A KNITTED CAST ON. THE MULTIPLE DIRECTIONS OF THE KNITTING AUTOMATICALLY PATTERNS ANY VARIEGATED YARN IN AN UNUSUAL WAY.

INSTRUCTIONS

Note: This sweater's construction method is to knit the Back, then instead of binding off for the shoulders, continue downward to knit the Front. Sleeves are knitted separately and then attached.

BACK

Cast on 100 (110, 120) sts.

Step 1

Make Closed Beginning Square.

With stitches already CO for base:

Row 1: Using the knitted cast on, CO 5 sts. K6, turn.

Row 2: S1, k1, turn.

Row 3: S1, k2, turn.

Row 4: S1, k1inc1, skp, turn.

Row 5: S1, k1inc1, k1, skp, turn.

Row 6: S1, k1, k1inc1, k1, skp, turn.

Row 7: S1, k1, k1inc1, k2, skp, turn.

Row 8: S1, k2, k1inc1, k2, skp, turn.

Row 9: S1, k2, k1inc1, k3, skp, turn.

Row 10: S1, k3, k1inc1, k3, skp, turn.

Row 11: S1, k3, k1inc1, *do not turn.*

Step 2

Make Cut-Out Squares.

Work 18 (20, 22).

Row 1: K2, bind off next 5 sts, place last st back on left-hand needle. Using the knitted cast on, CO 5 sts, turn, k1, pass last cast-on stitch over stitch just knitted, turn.

Row 2: S1, k1, k1inc1, k2, skp, turn.

Row 3: S1, k2, k1inc1, k2, skp, turn.

Row 4: S1, k2, k1inc1, k3, skp, turn.

Row 5: S1, k3, k1inc1, k3, skp, turn.

Row 6: S1, k3, k1inc, *do not turn.*

Step 3

Make Closed End Square.

Row 1: K5, turn.

Row 2: S1, k1, turn.

Row 3: S1, k2, turn.

Row 4: S1, k1inc1, skp, turn.

Row 5: S1, k1inc1, k1, skp, turn.

Row 6: S1, k1, k1inc1, k1, skp, turn.

MATERIALS

Approx total: 1104 (1380, 1656)yd/1008 (1260, 1512)m sport-weight wool yarn that knits up at 20 sts to 4"/10cm

Knitting needles: 4mm (size 6 U.S.)

Three ½"/1.3cm buttons

Sewing needle and matching thread

FINISHED MEASUREMENTS

Women's Sizes: S (M, L)

Chest: 39 (43, 47)"/99.1 (109.2, 119.4)cm

Length: 17 (19, 21)"/43.2 (48.3, 53.3)cm

GAUGE

One Unmitered Square = 1"/2.5cm wide x 1⅓"/3.3cm tall

Always take time to check your gauge.

PATTERN STITCHES

CENTER-INCREASE SQUARES
See page 51, and make a small practice swatch if you have never used this technique before.

Sleeve

CUT OUT KNITTING
See page 69, and make a small practice swatch if you have never used this technique before.

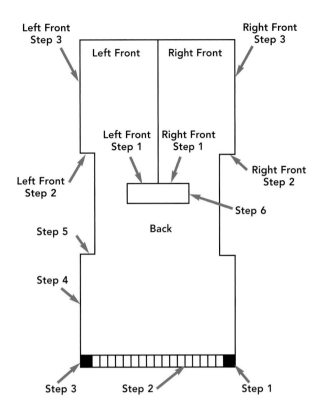

Left Front Step 3 | Right Front Step 3
Left Front | Right Front
Left Front Step 1 | Right Front Step 1
Left Front Step 2 | Right Front Step 2
Step 5 | Step 6
Back
Step 4
Step 3 | Step 2 | Step 1

Row 7: S1, k1, k1inc1, k2, skp, turn.

Row 8: S1, k2, k1inc1, k2, skp, turn.

Row 9: S1, k2, k1inc1, k3, skp, turn.

Row 10: S1, k3, k1inc1, k3, skp, turn.

Row 11: S1, k8, skp, turn.

Row 12: Bind off 5 sts. Slip last stitch back to left-hand needle.

Step 4

Work across entire row to return to beginning as follows:

K to end—100 (110, 120) sts; 20 (22, 24) squares across.

Repeat Steps 1 to 4, 10 (11, 12) more times—11 (12, 13) rows of squares completed.

Step 5

Make armholes.

BO 10 sts. Work 1 Closed Beginning Square, 14 (16, 18) Cut-Out Squares, and 1

Closed End Square. Turn and BO 10 sts, then k to end—80 (90, 100) sts; 16 (18, 20) total squares across.

Repeat five more times, but do not BO any more sts. For last row, end with k 20 (25, 30) sts, BO 40 sts, k 20 (25, 30) sts—20 (25, 30) sts in work on each side of Neck Opening.

Step 6

Work neck opening.

Place first 20 (25, 30) sts on stitch holder.

Work Closed Beginning Square, 2 (3, 4) Cut-Out Squares, and Closed End Square—4 (5, 6) squares, 20 (25, 30) sts across.

LEFT FRONT

Note: This side's squares will lay in the opposite direction from those of the back. Back and front are worked in one piece from back hem up and over shoulder and down to front hem.

Step 1

Work front collar.

K20 (25, 30) sts. Using the knitted cast on, CO 20 sts at neck edge. Work Closed Beginning Square, 6 (7, 8) Cut-Out Squares, and Closed End Square, then turn and k to end—40 (45, 50) sts; 8 (9, 10) squares across.

Repeat square pattern three more times for 3 rows of squares.

Step 2

Work armhole.

Work Closed Beginning Square, 6 (7, 8) Cut-Out Squares, and Closed End Square. Turn, then using the knitted cast on, CO 10. K to end—50 (55, 60) sts.

Step 3

Work body.

Work Closed Beginning Square, 8 (9, 10) Cut-Out Squares, and Closed End Square, then turn and k to end—50 (55, 60) sts, 10 (11, 12) squares across. Repeat square pattern 10 (11, 12) more times for 11 (12, 13) rows of squares from underarm. Length should equal Back.

BO 50 (55, 60) sts. Cut yarn.

Right Front

Transfer 20 sts from stitch holder onto needle.

Step 1

Work front collar.

Work Closed Beginning Square, 2 (3, 4) Cut-Out Squares, and Closed End Square. Turn and k to end—20 (25, 30) sts, 4 (5, 6) squares across. Using the knitted cast on, CO 20 sts.

Step 2

Work armhole.

Work Closed Beginning Square, 6 (7, 8) Cut-Out Squares, and Closed End Square—40 (45, 50) sts, 8 (9, 10) squares across. Turn and k to end. Repeat square pattern three more times for a total of 3 rows of squares.

Work Closed Beginning Square, 6 (7, 8) Cut-Out Squares, and Closed End Square. Then turn and k to end. Using the knitted cast on, CO 10 sts—50 (55, 60) sts in work.

Step 3

Work body.

Work Closed Beginning Square, 8 (9, 10) Cut-Out Squares, and Closed End Square. Then turn and k to end. Repeat square pattern 10 (11, 12) more times—11 (12, 13) rows of squares from underarm. Length should match Back.

BO 50 (55, 60) sts. Cut yarn.

Sleeves

Make 2.

CO 80 sts.

Note: Sleeve is knit from top down. You can optionally pick up 80 sts from the armhole edge.

Step 1

Begin sleeve—1st panel of Squares.

Panel 1: Work Closed Beginning Square, 14 Cut-Out Squares, and Closed End Square. Turn and k to end, decreasing 5 sts evenly across—75 sts.

Step 2

Work decreases—next 3 panels of Squares.

Panel 1: Work Closed Beginning Square, 13 Cut-Out Squares, and Closed End Square. Turn and k to end, decreasing 5 sts evenly across—70 sts.

Panel 2: Work Closed Beginning Square, 12 Cut-Out Squares, and Closed End Square. Turn and k to end, decreasing 5 sts evenly across—65 sts.

Panel 3: Work Closed Beginning Square, 11 Cut-Out Squares, and Closed End Square. Turn and k to end, decreasing 5 sts evenly across—60 sts.

Step 3

Work cuff.

K even for 8 rows.

BO all sts.

Repeat instructions to make a second sleeve.

Finishing

Sew each sleeve to armholes. Sew sleeve seams. Sew side seams.

Make I-Cord

Make a strand of I-cord 55"/140cm long. (See page 17 for instructions on making I-cord.) Thread the I-cord in and out around collar. Tie a knot in each end. To fasten the collar, tie the ends of the cord together.

Sew three buttons to left front, spacing them so that one is centered in first closed square at top of right front, the second is centered in third closed square beneath it, and the third is centered in the fifth closed square beneath it. Using a sewing needle and matching thread, form small button-holes in facing squares.

This sweater was knit with:
8 (10, 12) skeins of Artyarns Ultramerino 6, 100% merino wool, 1.8oz/50g = 138 yd/126m, color #101, variegated brown/gold/purple

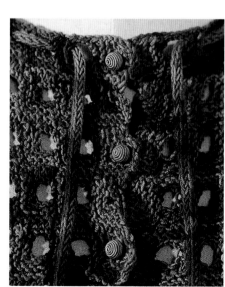

CENTER-DECREASE KNITTING
SHAPES

I N THIS CHAPTER YOU WILL LEARN TO KNIT SYMMETRICAL CENTER-DECREASE SHAPES THAT ARE BOUND OFF AND ATTACHED TO OTHER SHAPES WITH PICKED-UP STITCHES. THIS APPROACH IS MOST COMMONLY ASSOCIATED WITH MODULAR KNITTING.

Note: This method of modular knitting is covered widely in many books, and it is used here for only a few relatively simple projects. If you'd like to explore this technique further, refer to Vivian Hoxbro's *Domino Knitting*.

1 CENTER-DECREASE TRIANGLES

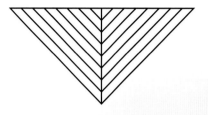

Figure 1

2 CENTER-DECREASE SQUARES

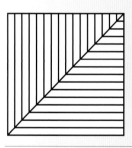

Figure 2

■ CENTER-DECREASE TRIANGLE

This shape is also known as a *Mitered Triangle*. Instead of *increasing* 4 stitches every 2 rows (as in the Center-Increase Triangle on page 51), in this Triangle you *decrease* 4 stitches every 2 rows except for the last row. The proportions of both triangles are similar.

Step 1

Using the knitted cast on, CO 23 sts.

Step 2

Make the Triangle.

Row 1: K22, p1.

Row 2: S1, k2tog, k7, s1, k2tog, psso, k7, k2tog, p1—19 sts.

Row 3: S1, k17, p1.

Row 4: S1, k2tog, k5, s1, k2tog, psso, k5, k2tog, p1—15 sts.

Row 5: S1, k13, p1.

Row 6: S1, k2tog, k3, s1, k2tog, psso, k3, k2tog, p1—11 sts.

Row 7: S1, k9, p1.

Row 8: S1, k2tog, k1, s1, k2tog, psso, k1, k2tog, p1—7 sts.

Row 9: S1, k5, p1.

Row 10: K2tog, s1, k2tog, psso, k2tog—3 sts.

Row 11: S1, k1, p1.

Row 12: S1, k2tog, psso—1 st.

■ CENTER-DECREASE SQUARE

This shape is also known as a *Mitered Square*. To knit this square, you decrease 2 stitches every 2 rows. This is the opposite of the Center-Increase Square on page 51 where you increase 2 stitches every 2 rows. Both shapes are therefore constructed in a similar manner. Slipping the first stitch and purling the last stitch of every row makes picking up stitches for subsequent shapes much easier.

Step 1

Using the knitted cast on, CO 23 sts.

Step 2

Row 1: K22, p1.

Row 2: S1, k9, s1, k2tog, psso, k9, p1—21 sts.

Row 3: S1, k19, p1.

Row 4: S1, k8, s1, k2tog, psso, k8, p1—19 sts.

Row 5: S1, k17, p1

Row 6: S1, k7, s1, k2tog, psso, k7, p1—17 sts.

Row 7: S1, k15, p1.

Row 8: S1, k6, s1, k2tog, psso, k6, p1—15 sts.

Row 9: S1, k13, p1.

Row 10: S1, k5, s1, k2tog, psso, k5, p1—13 sts.

Row 11: S1, k11, p1.

Row 12: S1, k4, s1, k2tog, psso, k4, p1—11 sts.

Row 13: S1, k9, p1.

Row 14: S1, k3, s1, k2tog, psso, k3, p1—9 sts.

Row 15: S1, k7, p1.

Row 16: S1, k2, s1, k2tog, psso, k2, p1—7 sts.

Row 17: S1, k5, p1.

Row 18: S1, k1, s1, k2tog, psso, k1, p1—5 sts.

Row 19: S1, k3, p1.

Row 20: S1, s1, k2tog, psso, p1—3 sts.

Row 21: S1, k2, p1.

Row 22: S1, k2tog, psso—1 st.

Adding Another Square

To add a second Center-Decrease Square as in figure 3, using the 1 remaining stitch, pick up 11 stitches along the side of Center-Decrease Square 1—12 sts. Then, use the knitted cast-on method to cast on 11 more sts—23 sts. Repeat rows 1 to 22.

Note: When you pick up stitches, insert the needle into both loops of the slipped-stitch edge. (See page 17 in Basics for instructions on picking up stitches.)

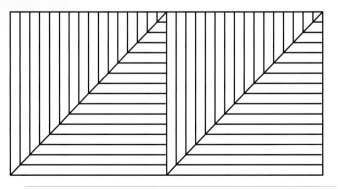

Figure 3

Center-Decrease Knitting Shapes

PINWHEEL PURSE

THIS SMALL PURSE IS THE PERFECT SIZE TO HOLD YOUR WALLET AND KEYS ON A TRIP TO THE MALL. MADE WITH JUST TWO BALLS OF YARN, THIS PROJECT IS AN INEXPENSIVE INTRODUCTION TO TRADITIONAL MODULAR KNITTING.

EXPERIENCE LEVEL ■ ■ INTERMEDIATE

MATERIALS

220yd/200m of worsted-weight wool blend yarn that knits up at 20 sts to 4"/10cm

Knitting needles: 5mm (size 8 U.S.) *or size to obtain gauge*

Crochet hook: 5mm (size H U.S.) for purse latch

1"/2.5cm round button

Tapestry needle

FINISHED MEASUREMENTS

10"/25.4cm width x 10"/25.4cm length (octagonal shape)

GAUGE

49 st and 24 row Mitered Triangle = 6 1/4"/15.9cm

Always take time to check your gauge.

PATTERN STITCH

CENTER-DECREASE TRIANGLES
See page 82, and make a small practice swatch if you have never used this technique before.

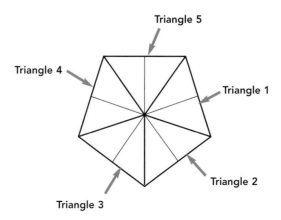

Triangle 5

Triangle 4

Triangle 1

Triangle 2

Triangle 3

INSTRUCTIONS

Step 1

Make Purse Back.

Triangle 1:

Using the knitted cast on, CO 49 sts.

Row 1: K48, p1.

Row 2: S1, k2tog, k20, s1, k2tog, psso, k20, k2tog, p1—45 sts.

Row 3: K44, p1.

Row 4: S1, k2tog, k18, s1, k2tog, psso, k18, k2tog, p1—41 sts.

Row 5: K40, p1.

Row 6: S1, k2tog, k16, s1, k2tog, psso, k16, k2tog, p1—37 sts.

Row 7: K36, p1.

Row 8: S1, k2tog, k14, s1, k2tog, psso, k14, k2tog, p1—33 sts.

Row 9: K32, p1.

Row 10: S1, k2tog, k12, s1, k2tog, psso, k12, k2tog, p1—29 sts.

Row 11: K28, p1.

Row 12: S1, k2tog, k10, s1, k2tog, psso, k10, k2tog, p1—25 sts.

Row 13: K24, p1.

Row 14: S1, k2tog, k8, s1, k2tog, psso, k8, k2tog, p1—21 sts.

Row 15: K20, p1.

Row 16: S1, k2tog, k6, s1, k2tog, psso, k6, k2tog, p1—17 sts.

Row 17: K16, p1.

Row 18: S1, k2tog, k4, s1, k2tog, psso, k4, k2tog, p1—13 sts.

Row 19: K12, p1.

Row 20: S1, k2tog, k2, s1, k2tog, psso, k2, k2tog, p1—9 sts.

Row 21: K8, p1.

Row 22: S1, k2tog, s1, k2tog, psso, k2tog, p1—5 sts.

Row 23: K4, p1.

Row 24: BO 5 sts, cut yarn.

Triangles 2 to 5: Starting at bottom point of previously completed triangle, pick up 25 sts along one side of the triangle. Using the knitted cast on, CO 24 sts.

Repeat rows 1 to 24. After 5 triangles are complete, sew side of Triangle 5 to side of Triangle 1 to form octagonal shape.

Step 2

Make Purse Front.

Triangle 1: Repeat instructions for Triangle 1 in Step 1.

Triangles 2 to 4: Repeat instructions for Triangles 2 to 5 in Step 1. All 4 triangles are now attached.

Triangle 5: Make this triangle separately for Purse Flap by repeating instructions for Triangle 1.

FINISHING

Purse Flap

Thread yarn through tapestry needle and sew top side of Triangle 5 of Purse Front to one side of the octagon of the purse back.

Purse Latch

Using crochet hook, pull loop through bottom point of Triangle 5 of Purse Front, and chain 8, joining 8th chain to the first with single crochet. Continue and sc 16 into the loop just formed, joining the last sc to the first with a slip stitch. Cut yarn, weave in ends.

Attach Purse Front to Back

Turn fabric so wrong side faces out, thread yarn through tapestry needle, and sew purse front to purse back on 4 sides where they align. Turn bag so right side is facing out.

Sew button at top of intersection of Triangles 2 and 3 of Purse Front.

Purse Straps

Make two 24"/61cm I-cord straps (see instructions on page 15).

Using the photo as a guide, attach the ends of one strap to the front of the purse on the sides of the front flap. Push the ends of the strap through the knitting to the inside of the purse, and tie a knot to hold the strap in place.

Repeat with the other strap on the back of the purse.

Hide the knots by sewing approx 1"/2.5cm of the sides of the front opening to the back of the purse.

Sew button to center front of bag.

Cut yarn, weave in ends.

THIS PURSE WAS KNIT WITH:

2 BALLS OF NORO'S SILK GARDEN, 45% SILK/45% KID MOHAIR/10% LAMB'S WOOL, APPROX 1.8OZ/50G = 110YDS/100M, COLOR #86

ZEBRA AFGHAN

THIS ZEBRA-STRIPED AFGHAN IS JUST THE RIGHT SIZE TO COVER YOUR LAP WHILE WATCHING TV OR TO WRAP AROUND YOUR SHOULDERS WHILE READING. IT'S ALSO SMALL ENOUGH FOR A COLLEGE DORM ROOM. THE ZIGZAG STRIPE DESIGN WILL WAKE UP THE DECOR IN ANY ROOM. FOR A QUIETER VERSION, TRY USING TWO SHADES OF ONE COLOR.

EXPERIENCE LEVEL ■■ INTERMEDIATE

MATERIALS

Approx total: 1680yd/1536m of worsted-weight wool or wool blend yarn that knits up at 20 sts to 4"/10cm

Color A: 840yds/768m in white

Color B: 840yds/768m in black

Knitting needles: 5.5mm (Size 9 U.S.) *or size to obtain gauge*

Crochet hook: 5mm (size H U.S.) for attaching trim

FINISHED MEASUREMENTS

28"/71.1cm wide x 42"/106.7cm long without trim

GAUGE

49 st x 48 row Mitered Square = 7"/17.8cm

Always take time to check your gauge.

PATTERN STITCH

CENTER-DECREASE SQUARES
See page 83, and make a small practice swatch if you have never used this technique before.

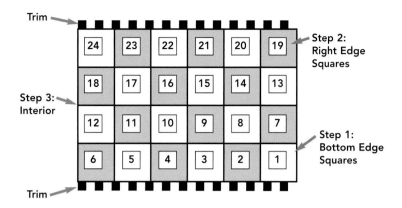

Trim

24 23 22 21 20 19 → Step 2: Right Edge Squares

18 17 16 15 14 13

Step 3: Interior → 12 11 10 9 8 7

6 5 4 3 2 1 → Step 1: Bottom Edge Squares

Trim →

Note: This pattern uses two types of mitered squares. None of the rows are knit in a single color—they all use one color for the first half of the row, and another color for the second half. You also change colors after every 6 rows.

1. The White Center-Decrease Square is actually half white and half black, starting out with a white edge on the right-hand side, followed by a black edge on the bottom of the square. Every 6 rows the colors are transposed.

2. The Black Center-Decrease Square is actually half black and half white, starting out with a black edge on the right-hand side of the square, followed by a white edge on the bottom of the square. Every 6 rows the colors are transposed.

Because every square is knit similarly, and the only thing that changes is the starting yarn color, please use this as a guide:

White Square: A=Yarn A, B=Yarn B

Black Square: A=Yarn B, B=Yarn A

INSTRUCTIONS

Note on changing yarn colors: At all times you will be working one color yarn on one half of the row and another color yarn on the second half of the row. Carry the unused strand on the wrong side of the work. Twist A and B whenever you change colors to ensure that no holes form and to keep the work neat on both sides.

Note on cutting yarn: After each square is complete, continue working with the color specified, and cut the other color yarn. Attach it at the point where it is required. You can weave in the short tail while you knit, or you can weave in all the ends after you finish knitting. When you have completed a row of squares, cut both strands.

Step 1

Make Bottom Edge Squares 1 to 6.

Square 1 (White Square):

Using A and the knitted cast on, CO 25 sts. Drop A, attach B. With B, cast on 24 more sts.

Row 1 (WS): With B, k24, drop B, pick up A, keeping strands in front. With A, k24, p1—49 sts.

Row 2 (RS): S1, with A, k21, s1, k2tog, psso, drop A. With B, k22, p1.

Row 3: S1, with B, k22, drop B, pick up A, keeping strands in front. With A, k23, p1—47 sts.

Row 4: S1, with A, k21, s1, k2tog, psso, drop A. With B, k21, p1.

Row 5: S1, with, B k43, p1—45 sts.

Row 6: S1, with B, k20, s1, k2tog, psso. Drop B, pick up A. With A, k20, p1.

Row 7: S1, with A, k20. Drop A, pick up B. With B, k21, p1—43 sts.

Row 8: S1, with B, k19, s1, k2tog, psso. Drop B, pick up A. With A, k19, p1.

Row 9: S1, with A, k19. Drop A, pick up B. With B, k20, p1—41 sts.

Row 10: S1, with B, k18, s1, k2tog, psso. Drop B, pick up A. With A, k18, p1.

Row 11: S1, with A, k37, p1—39 sts.

Row 12: S1, with A, k17, s1, k2tog, psso. Drop A, pick up B. With B, k17, p1.

Rows 13 to 48: Continue working in pattern, changing starting color every 6 rows, knitting 1 st less before and after the center s1, k2tog, psso on each even row, making sure to switch to second color immediately after the double decrease, and on the odd row knit the colors as they face you. When you have 1 st left, cut A.

Squares 2, 4, and 6 (Black Squares):

With B, pick up 24 more sts along left side of square immediately to the right of the one you are working. Attach A. Using the knitted cast on, CO 24 sts.

Repeat rows 1 to 48, substituting B wherever A is called, and A wherever B is called. Cut B. (Cut both A and B when completing Square 6.)

Squares 3 and 5 (White Squares):

With A, pick up 24 more sts along left side of square immediately to the right of the one you are working. Attach B. Using the knitted cast on, CO 24 sts.

Repeat rows 1 to 48, using Yarn A wherever A is called, and Yarn B wherever B is called. Cut A.

Step 2

Make Right Edge Squares.

Square 7, Black Square: Using B and the knitted cast on, CO 25 sts. Drop B, attach A, and pick up 24 sts along the top of Square 1.

Repeat rows 1 to 48, using Yarn B wherever A is called, and Yarn A wherever B is called.

Cut A and B.

Square 13, White Square: Using A and the knitted cast on, CO 25 sts. Drop A, attach B, and pick up 24 sts along the top of Square 7.

Repeat rows 1 to 48, using Yarn A wherever A is called and Yarn B wherever B is called.

Cut A and B.

Square 19, Black Square: Using B and the knitted cast on, CO 25 sts. Drop

B, attach A, and pick up 24 sts along the top of Square 13.

Repeat rows 1 to 48, using Yarn B wherever A is called and Yarn A wherever B is called.

Cut A and B.

Step 3

Make Interior Squares.

Square 8, White Square: With A, pick up 24 more sts along left edge of Square 7. Drop A, attach B. With B, pick up 24 sts along top edge of Square 2. Repeat rows 1 to 48 using Yarn A wherever A is called and Yarn B wherever B is called.

Square 9, Black Square: With B, pick up 24 more sts along left edge of Square 8. Drop B, attach A. With A, pick up 24 sts along top edge of Square 3. Repeat rows 1 to 48 using Yarn B wherever A is called and Yarn A wherever B is called.

Square 10, White Square: With A, pick up 24 more sts along left edge of Square 9. Drop A, attach B. With B, pick up 24 sts along top edge of Square 4. Repeat rows 1 to 48 using Yarn A wherever A is called and Yarn B wherever B is called.

Square 11, Black Square: With B, pick up 24 more sts along left edge of Square 10. Drop B, attach A. With A, pick up 24 sts along top edge of Square 5. Repeat rows 1 to 48 using Yarn B wherever A is called and Yarn A wherever B is called.

Square 12, White Square: With A, pick up 24 more sts along left edge of

Square 11. Drop A, attach B. With B, pick up 24 sts along top edge of Square 6. Repeat rows 1 to 48 using Yarn A wherever A is called and Yarn B wherever B is called. Cut A and B.

Continue adding interior squares (squares 14 to 18, and squares 20 to 24) in this fashion, making sure to alternate White Squares with Black Squares. Follow diagram for placement, and repeat rows 1 to 48 using Yarn A whenever A is called and Yarn B wherever B is called for White Squares, and vice versa.

FINISHING

Make Loopy Trim

Using both A and B yarns together, take crochet hook and insert into rightmost corner stitch of Square 1. ★Pull loop and wrap loop 1 time around left thumb. Leaving loop wrapped around thumb, take crochet hook and secure loop with a single crochet into stitch to the left of the stitch just worked. Insert crochet hook into the stitch to the left of the stitch just worked. Repeat from ★ across bottom edge of blanket. Cut yarn, and repeat on top edge of blanket.

Cut yarn. Weave in all ends.

THIS AFGHAN WAS KNIT WITH:

JAGGERSPUN'S ZEPHYR WOOL/SILK 4/8, 50% WOOL/50% SILK, 4OZ/113G = 280YDS/256M PER SKEIN

(A) 3 SKEINS COLOR VANILLA

(B) 3 SKEINS COLOR EBONY

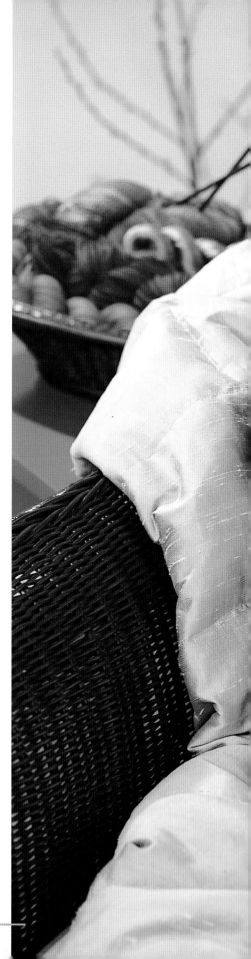

HIDDEN SQUARE PILLOW

WHETHER YOU DISPLAY IT WITH OTHER DECORATIVE PILLOWS ON YOUR SOFA, OR LET IT SPEAK FOR ITSELF ON AN EXQUISITE CHAIR, THIS PILLOW IS SURE TO DAZZLE. THE MITERED SQUARES ARE KNIT HALF IN ONE COLOR AND HALF IN THE OTHER, AND THE UNUSED YARN IS PASSED OVER THE CENTER OF THE SQUARE, MAKING IT REVERSIBLE SHOULD YOU CHOOSE TO MODIFY THE PROJECT AND MAKE AN AFGHAN OR SCARF.

MATERIALS

Approx total: 478yd/430m DK-weight wool yarn that knits up at approx 22 sts to 4"/10cm

Color A: 239yd/218.5m in red

Color B: 239yd/218.5m in blue

Knitting needles: 3.75mm (Size 5 U.S.) *or size to obtain gauge*

Three 1"/2.5cm wooden buttons

14"/35.6cm square pillow form

FINISHED MEASUREMENTS

15" square/38.1 cm

GAUGE

25 st and 24 row Mitered Square = 2½"/6.4cm

19 sts and 42 rows = 4"/10cm in Garter Stitch

Always take time to check your gauge.

PATTERN STITCH

CENTER-DECREASE SQUARES
See page 83, and make a small practice swatch if you have never used this technique before.

Note: Squares where the right side starts with color A (red) and the left side ends with color B (blue) are called Red Squares. Squares where the right side starts with Color B (blue) and the left side ends with color A (red) are called Blue Squares. This pillow is constructed in 4 quadrants that are sewn together to mirror one another and create a symmetrical pattern.

INSTRUCTIONS

Note on changing yarn colors:
At all times you will be working one color yarn on one half of the row and another color yarn on the second half of the row. Twist A and B on every row on the wrong side of the work whenever you change colors to ensure that no holes form and to keep the work neat on both sides.

Note on cutting yarn: After each square is complete, continue working with the color specified, and cut the other color yarn. Attach it at the point where it is required. You can weave in the short tail while you knit, or you can weave in all the ends after you finish knitting. When you have completed a row of squares, cut both strands.

Step 1

Make Quadrant 1.

Square 1 (Red Square):

With A, using the knitted cast on, CO 13 sts. Drop A, attach B. With B, using knitted cast on, CO 12 sts—25 sts.

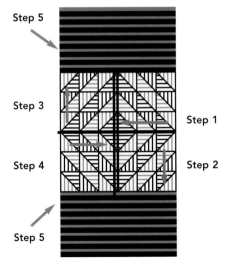

Note: Follow arrow for start point and direction of knitting

Row 1 (WS): K.

Row 2: S1, with A, k10, s1, k2tog, psso. Drop A, pick up B. With B, k10, p1—23 sts.

Row 3: S1, with B, k10, with A, k11, p1.

Row 4: S1, with A, k9, s1, k2tog, psso. Drop A, pick up B. With B, k9, p1—21 sts.

Row 5: S1, with B, k9, with A, k10, p1.

Row 6: S1, with A, k8, s1, k2tog, psso. Drop A, pick up B. With B, k8, p1—19 sts.

Row 7: S1, with B, k8, with A, k9, p1.

Row 8: S1, with A, k7, s1, k2tog, psso. Drop A, pick up B. With B, k7, p1—17 sts.

Row 9: S1, with B, k7, with A, k8, p1.

Rows 10 to 22: Continue working in pattern, knitting 1 st less before and after the center s1, k2tog, psso on each even row until 3 sts remain.

Row 23: S1, with B, k1, with A, p1. Cut A.

Row 24: With B, s1, k2tog, psso—1 st.

Square 2 (Blue Square):

With B, pick up 12 more sts along left side of Square 1. Attach A. Using the knitted cast on, CO 12 sts—25 sts.

Repeat rows 1 to 24, substituting B wherever A is called, and A wherever B is called. Cut B.

Square 3 (Red Square):

With A, pick up 12 more sts along left side of Square 2. Attach B. Using the knitted cast on, CO 12 sts—25 sts.

Repeat rows 1 to 24. Cut A and B.

Square 4 (Blue Square):

With B, using knitted cast on, CO 13. Drop B, attach A. Pick up 12 sts from top of Square 1—25 sts.

Repeat rows 1 to 24, substituting B wherever A is called, and A wherever B is called. Cut B .

Square 5 (Red Square):

With A, pick up 13 sts along left side of Square 4. Attach B. Pick up 12 sts from top of Square 2—25 sts.

Repeat rows 1 to 24. Cut A.

Square 6 (Blue Square):

With B, pick up 12 more sts along left side of Square 5. Attach A. Pick up 12 sts from top of Square 3—25 sts.

Repeat rows 1 to 24, substituting B wherever A is called, and A wherever B is called. Cut A and B.

Square 7 (Red Square):

With A, using the knitted cast on, CO 13 sts. Attach B. Pick up 12 sts from top of Square 4—25 sts.

Repeat rows 1 to 24.

Square 8 (Blue Square):

With B, pick up 12 sts along left side of Square 7. Attach A. Pick up 12 sts from top of Square 5—25 sts.

Repeat rows 1 to 24, substituting B wherever A is called, and A wherever B is called.

Square 9 (Red Square):

With A, pick up 12 more sts along left side of Square 8. Attach B. Pick up 12 sts from top of Square 6—25 sts.

Repeat rows 1 to 24.

Steps 2 and 3

Make Quadrants 2 and 3.

Repeat Step 1, substituting all Blue Squares for Red Squares, and all Red Squares for Blue Squares.

Step 4

Make Quadrant 4.

Repeat Step 1.

Sew the 4 quadrants together as shown in diagram, so they form a diamond pattern.

Step 5

Make Back Panels.

Panel 1:

With RS facing and A, pick up 72 sts along bottom of fabric.

Row 1: K.

Rows 2 to 4: K.

Drop A, attach B.

Row 5: K.

Rows 6 to 8: K.

Drop B, attach A .

Row 9: K.

Repeat rows 2 to 9 ten times, ending with row 9. With A, bind off all stitches.

Panel 2:

With RS facing and A, pick up 72 sts along opposite end of pillow.

Repeat instructions for Back Panel 1.

Next 4 rows: With B, K.

Next row (buttonholes): K16, bo3, k16, bo3, k16, bo3, k16, bo3, k15.

Next row: K15, ★using knitted cast on, CO 3, k16; rep from ★ to end.

Next row: Knit.

Next row: Bind off all sts.

FINISHING

Cut yarn, weave in ends.

Sew buttons in position on opposite back panel so that they fit directly into buttonholes. Turn pillow inside out. Sew sides, overlapping flaps by ¼"/6mm. Place pillow form inside pillow. Close buttons.

THIS PILLOW WAS KNIT WITH:

2 BALLS OF DAIKETO'S DIAMUSEEFINE, 100% WOOL, APPROX 1.4OZ/40G = 239 YD/219M PER BALL

(A) 1 BALL COLOR #113 RED

(B) 1 BALL COLOR #106 BLUE

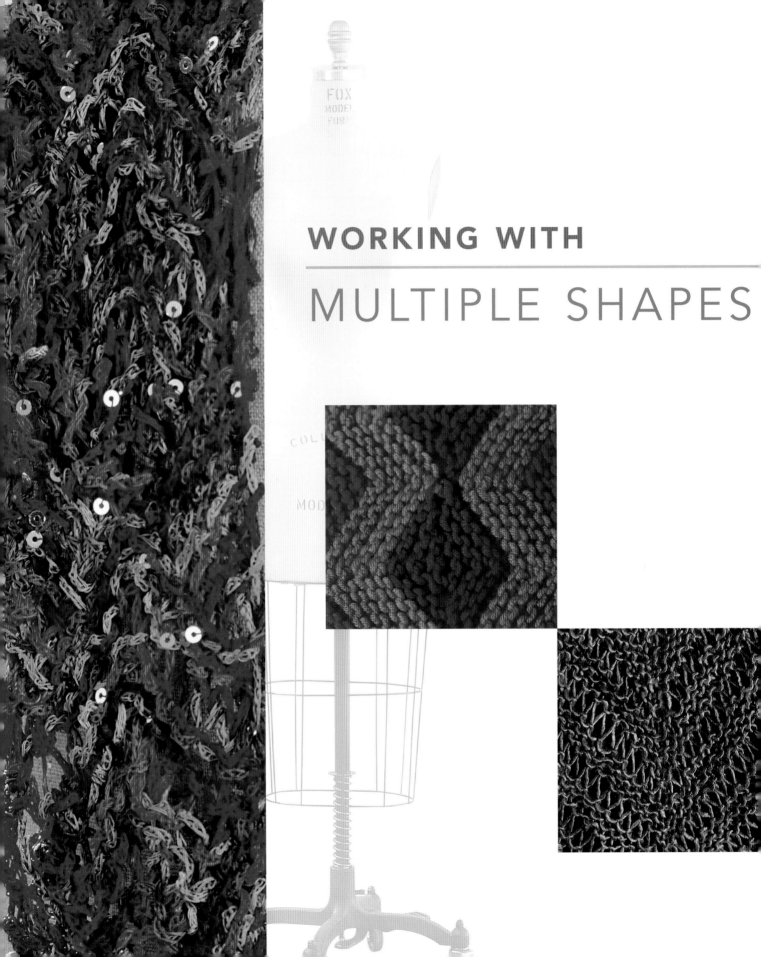

WORKING WITH

MULTIPLE SHAPES

I N THIS CHAPTER YOU WILL FIND MANY INTERMEDIATE AND ADVANCED PROJECTS KNIT WITH MULTIPLE MODULAR SHAPES. KNITTING MODULES FREES YOUR CREATIVITY, EVEN WHEN YOU ARE ONLY WORKING WITH ONE SHAPE AT A TIME. WHEN YOU COMBINE SHAPES, THE POSSIBILITIES ARE INFINITE. THE PROJECTS ON THE FOLLOWING PAGES WILL GIVE YOU A STARTING POINT. SOON YOU WILL BE DESIGNING YOUR OWN UNIQUE PIECES.

DIAMOND BLOSSOM SCARF

SILK RIBBON AND FUR YARN COMBINE TO GIVE THIS PLEASANT SCARF SPARKLY SHEEN AND SOFT DRAPE. THIS IS AN ALL-SEASON ACCESSORY THAT YOU WILL FIND YOURSELF REACHING FOR WHENEVER YOU WANT TO SPICE UP YOUR WARDROBE.

INSTRUCTIONS

Step 1

Make 2 Base Triangles.

Using the knitted cast on, CO 11 sts.

Row 1: K1inc1, k1, turn; pm, s1, k2, turn.

Row 2: K1inc1, k to marker, rm, k1, turn; pm, s1, k to end, turn.

Repeat row 2 until all 11 cast-on sts have been used up, ending with: k1inc1, k to marker, rm, k1—21 sts, *do not turn.*

Repeat instructions for Base Triangle to make a facing Base Triangle on the other side. There will be 21 sts on the right needle and 21 sts on the left needle. *Do not turn.*

Step 2

Make a Diamond.

Row 1: K1, turn.

Row 2: S1, k2, turn.

Row 3: S1, k1inc1, skp, turn.

Row 4: S1, k1inc1, pm1, k1, skp, turn.

Row 5: S1, pm2, k to marker 1, rm1, k1inc1, pm1, k1, skp, turn.

Row 6: S1, pm3, k to marker 1, rm1, k1inc1, pm1, k to marker 2, rm2, skp, turn.

Row 7: S1, pm2 , k to marker 1, rm1, k1inc1, pm1, k to marker 3, rm3, skp, turn.

Continue to repeat rows 6 and 7 and end with row 6 when you have 8 unworked stitches on the other side of marker 2.

Last row: S1, k to marker 1, rm1, k1inc1, k to marker 3, rm3, skp, *do not turn;* k8, turn.

Step 3

Enclose the Diamond in the Diagonal Knitting.

Side 1:

Row 1: K1inc1, k6, skp, turn.

Row 2: S1, pm, k to end, turn.

Row 3: K1inc1, k to marker, rm, skp, turn.

Repeat rows 2 and 3 until you have 20 sts on the right needle. Repeat row 2 once more.

EXPERIENCE LEVEL ■ ■ INTERMEDIATE

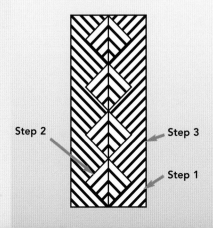

Step 2

Step 3

Step 1

Repeat rows 2 and 3 until you have 20 sts on the right needle. Repeat row 2 once more.

Next row: K1inc1, k to marker, rm, skp, *do not turn;* k21—42 sts, turn.

Side 2:

Follow instructions for Side 1, repeating rows 1 to 3 once, then rows 2 and 3 until there are 20 sts on the right needle. Repeat row 2 one final time.

Last row: K1inc1, k to marker, rm, skp, *do not turn.*

Alternate Steps 2 and 3, ending with Step 2 when scarf is 48"/122cm or desired length.

Step 4

Make Ending Triangles.

Row 1: K1inc1, k6, skp, turn; s1, k to end, turn.

Row 2: K1inc1, k7, skp, turn; s1, k to end, turn.

Row 3: K1inc1, k8, skp, turn; s1, k9, s1wyif, turn.

Row 4: Skp, k8, skp, turn; s1, k8, s1wyif, turn.

Row 5: Skp, k7, skp, turn; s1, k7, s1wyif, turn.

Row 6: Skp, k6, skp, turn; s1, k6, s1wyif, turn.

Row 7: Skp, k5, skp, turn; s1, k5, s1wyif, turn.

Row 8: Skp, k4, skp, turn; s1, k4, s1wyif, turn.

Row 9: Skp, k3, skp, turn; s1, k3, s1wyif, turn.

Row 10: Skp, k2, skp, turn; s1, k2, s1wyif, turn.

Row 11: Skp, k1, skp, turn; s1, k1, s1wyif, turn.

Row 12: Skp, skp, pass 2nd st on right needle over 1st, k1, pass 2nd st on right needle over 1st, then bind off 1 more stitch. K21.

Repeat rows 1 to 11 for other side. End as follows:

Last row: Skp, skp, pass 2nd st on right needle over 1st, k1, pass 2nd st on right needle over 1st, and bind off last stitch.

FINISHING

Fur Trim

Using crochet hook and fur yarn, single crochet into each of the stitches on one end of the scarf. Work 3 more rows of single crochet. Repeat on other end of scarf.

Cut yarn, weave in ends.

THIS SCARF WAS KNIT WITH:

(A) 2 SKEINS ARTYARNS SILK RIBBON, 100% SILK, APPROX 0.9OZ/25G = 128YDS/117M PER SKEIN, COLOR #123

(B) 1 SKEIN ARTYARNS SILK FUR, 90% SILK/10% NYLON, APPROX 0.9OZ/44M = 48YDS/44M PER SKEIN, COLOR #123

SEQUINED
EVENING
SASH

SEQUINED YARN
AND TASSELS
ADD FLAIR TO
THIS QUICK-TO-KNIT
SASH. IT'S RIGHT IN
STYLE, EITHER WORN
AS A NECK SCARF WITH
A COCKTAIL DRESS, OR
SLUNG LOW AROUND
THE HIPS WITH BELL-
BOTTOM BLUE JEANS.

MATERIALS

Approx total: 180yd/165m DK-weight yarn that knits up at 22 sts to 4"/10cm

Knitting needles: 5mm (size 8 U.S.) *or size to obtain gauge*

Crochet hook: 3.5mm (size E U.S.) for attaching tassels

FINISHED MEASUREMENTS

3"/7.6cm wide x 42"/106.7cm long

GAUGE

Single Diamond Panel = 3"/7.6cm wide x 3"/7.6cm long

Always take time to check your gauge.

PATTERN STITCHES

DIAGONAL SIDE TRIANGLES
See page 28, and make a small practice swatch if you have never used this technique before.

CENTER-INCREASE DIAMONDS
See page 51, and make a small practice swatch if you have never used this technique before.

OPENWORK
Work a yo between each knit stitch as indicated in pattern. Do not work a yo in the middle of k1inc1.

On the next row, drop the yarn overs to create elongated stitches.

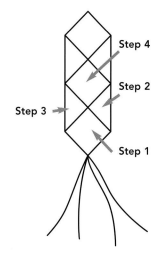

INSTRUCTIONS

Cast on 2 sts.

Step 1

Make Diamond 1.

Row 1 (RS): K1inc1, k1, turn—3 sts.

Row 2 (WS): K1inc1, k1inc1, k1, turn—5 sts.

Row 3: K1inc1, k1inc1, k2, p1, turn—7 sts.

Row 4: Adding a yo between every stitch in this row, s1, k2, k1inc1, k2, p1, turn.

Row 5: Dropping each yo that was added in the previous, s1, k2, k1inc1, k3, p1, turn—9 sts.

Row 6: S1, k3, k1inc1, k3, p1, turn—10 sts.

Row 7: Adding a yo between every stitch in this row, s1, k3, k1inc1, k4, p1, turn.

Row 8: : Dropping each yo that was added in the previous row, s1, k4, k1inc1, k4, p1, turn—12 sts.

Row 9: S1, k4, k1inc1, k5, p1, turn—13 sts.

Row 10: S1, k5, k1inc1, k5, p1, turn—14 sts.

Row 11: Adding a yo between every stitch in this row, s1, k5, k1inc1, k6, p1, turn.

Row 12: Dropping each yo that was added in the previous row, s1, k6, k1inc1, k6, p1, turn—16 sts.

Row 13: S1, k6, k1inc1, k7, p1, turn—17 sts.

Row 14: S1, k7, k1inc1, k7, p1, turn—18 sts.

Step 2

Make Triangle 1.

Row 1: K1inc1, skp, turn; s1, k2, turn.

Row 2: K1inc1, k1, skp, turn; s1, k3, turn.

Row 3: K1inc1, k2, skp, turn; s1, k4, turn.

Row 4: K1inc1, k3, skp, turn; s1, k5, turn.

Row 5: K1inc1, k4, skp, turn; s1, k6, turn.

Row 6: K1inc1, k5, skp, turn; s1, k7, turn.

Row 7: Kinc1, k6, skp, k9, turn.

Step 3

Make Triangle 2.

Repeat rows 1 to 6 of Triangle 1.

Next row: K1inc1, k6, skp, *do not turn.*

Step 4

Make Diamond 2.

Row 1: K1, turn.

Row 2: S1, k2, turn.

Row 3: S1, k1inc1, skp, turn.

Row 4: S1, k1inc1, k1, skp, turn.

Row 5: Adding a yo between every stitch in this row, s1, k1, k1inc1, yo, k1, skp, turn.

Row 6: Dropping each yo that was added in the previous row, s1, k1, k1inc1, k2, skp, turn.

Row 7: S1, k2, k1inc1, k2, skp, turn.

Row 8: S1, k2, k1inc1, k3, skp, turn.

Row 9: Adding a yo between every stitch in this row, s1, k3, k1inc1, k3, skp, turn.

Row 10: Dropping each yo that was added in the previous row, s1, k3, k1inc1, k4, skp, turn.

Row 11: S1, k4, k1inc1, k4, skp, turn.

Row 12: S1, k4, k1inc1, k5, skp, turn.

Row 13: Adding a yo between every stitch in this row, s1, k5, k1inc1, k5, skp, turn.

Row 14: Dropping each yo that was added in the previous row, s1, k5, k1inc1, k6, skp, turn.

Row 15: S1, k6, k1inc1, k6, skp, turn.

Row 16: S1, k6, k1inc1, k7, skp, turn.

Row 17: S1, k7, k1inc1, k7, skp, turn.

Repeat steps 2 to 4 until sash is desired length.

Bind off all sts.

FINISHING

Cut yarn, weave in ends. Attach tassels, one to each end as follows.

Making Tassels

Cut thirty 12"/30.5cm lengths of yarn.

Cut two 16"/40.6cm lengths of yarn.

Combine half of the strands (fifteen 12"/30.5cm lengths, and one 16"/40.6cm length) for the first tassel. Insert a large crochet hook into the center stitch of the bound-off stitches at the end of the knitted scarf. Draw the cut strands through this stitch, making sure that the 12"/30.5cm strands are hanging evenly on both sides of the stitch. Wrap the 16"/40.6cm strand around the 12"/30.5cm strands 5 times. Insert a crochet hook upwards into the tassel, catch the 16"/40.6cm strand that has been wrapping around the tassel, and pull it through so that it is hanging down with the remaining 12"/30.5cm strands. Trim if necessary to even lengths.

Repeat on other end of scarf with remaining strands of tassel yarn.

THIS SASH WAS KNIT WITH:

2 SKEINS OF GREAT ADIRONDACK'S SEQUINS, 90% RAYON/10% POLYESTER, 100YD/91.4M, COLOR TOUCAN

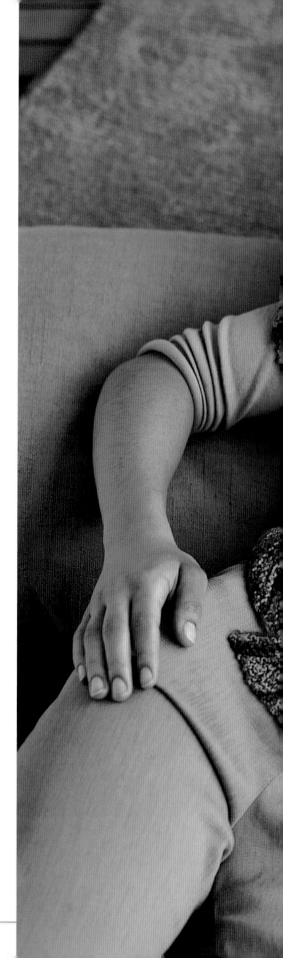

SHEER ONE-PIECE SHAWL

THIS LOVELY SHAWL IS SHAPED TO WRAP AROUND YOUR SHOULDERS WITH A FLATTERING DRAPE. PERFECT FOR COOL SUMMER EVENINGS OR AIR-CONDITIONED BUILDINGS, THE SHEER TEXTURE IS FORMED BY SIMPLY PLACING YARN OVERS BETWEEN STITCHES ON ONE PATTERN ROW AND DROPPING THEM ON THE NEXT, TO CREATE ELONGATED STITCHES THAT LOOK LIKE COMPLICATED LACE.

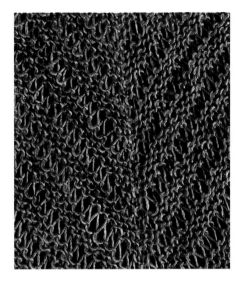

INSTRUCTIONS

Note: The shawl is worked in one continuous piece, starting with Diamond 1, then Diamond 2, then Diamond 3, then Triangle 4, and ending with Triangle 5.

Cast on 2 sts.

Step 1

Make Diamond 1.

Row 1: K1inc1, k1, turn—3 sts.

Row 2: K1inc1, k1inc1, k1, turn—5 sts.

Row 3: K1inc1, k1inc1, pm, k2, p1, turn—7 sts.

Rows 4 to 6: S1, k to marker, rm, k1inc1, pm, k to last 1 st, p1, turn.

Row 7: S1, *yo, k1; rep from * to marker, rm, yo, k1inc1, pm *yo, k1, rep to last 1 st, p1, turn.

Row 8: Dropping all yo's, s1, k to marker, rm, k1inc1, pm, k1, k to last 1 st, p1, turn.

Rows 9 to 12: S1, k to marker, rm, k1inc1, pm, k to last 1 st, p1, turn.

Rep rows 7 to 12 until one side of the diamond measures approx 10"/25.4cm to 12"/30.5cm (small/medium) or 14"/35.6cm to 20"/50.8cm (large/extra-large).

Note: This Diamond should cover your entire back and should extend from the neck down as far as you'd like the shawl to reach. To make the shawl larger, continue repeating rows 7 to 12 until the diamond is the desired size.

Last row: S1, k to marker, rm, k1inc1, pm, k to end, turn.

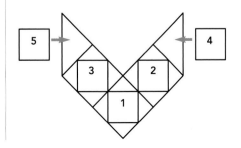

MATERIALS

Approx total: 525yd/480m (1050yd/960m) worsted-weight yarn that knits up at 20 sts to 4"/10cm

Knitting needles: 4.5mm (size 7 U.S.) *or size to obtain gauge*

3 stitch markers

FINISHED MEASUREMENTS

Small/Medium (Large/Extra-Large)

Side of the center-back Diamond measures approx 10"/25.4cm to 12"/30.5cm (small/medium) or 14"/35.6cm to 20"/50.8cm (large/extra-large)

GAUGE

15 st x 15 row Unmitered Square = 4 x 4"/10 x 10cm square in Pattern Stitch

Always take time to check your gauge.

PATTERN STITCHES

DIAGONAL TRIANGLES

See page 28, and make a small practice swatch if you have never used this technique before.

CENTER-INCREASE SQUARES

See page 51, and make a small practice swatch if you have never used this technique before.

OPENWORK PARTITION

Work a yo between each knit stitch as indicated in pattern.

On the next row, drop the yarn overs to create elongated stitches.

Step 2

Make Diamond 2.

Following the order in the diagram on page 107, end at one of the corners of Diamond 1 and begin Diamond 2 as follows:

Row 1: K1inc1, turn; s1, k1, turn—2 sts.

Row 2: K1inc1, skp, turn; s1, k1inc1, p1—4 sts.

Row 3: S1, k1inc1, k1, skp, turn—5 sts.

Row 4: S1, pm, k1, k1inc1, pm, k1, p1, turn.

Row 5: S1, k to marker, rm, k1inc1, pm, k to marker, rm, skp, turn.

Row 6: S1, pm, k to marker, rm, k1inc1, pm, k to last 1 st, p1, turn.

Row 7: S1, *yo, k1; rep from * to marker, rm, yo, k1inc1, pm *yo, k1, rep to marker, rm, yo, skp, turn.

Row 8: Dropping all yo's, s1, pm, k to marker, rm, k1inc1, pm, k to last 1 st, p1, turn.

Rows 9 and 11: S1, k to marker, rm, k1inc1, pm, k to marker, rm, skp, turn.

Rows 10 and 12: S1, pm, k to marker, rm, k1inc1, pm, k to last 1 st, p1, turn.

Rep rows 7 to 12 until you have reached the marker on previously knitted Diamond 1. Remove marker. Work the last 2 rows of Diamond 2 as follows:

Row 1: S1, pm, k to marker, rm, k1inc1, pm, k to last 1 st, p1, turn.

Row 2: S1, k to marker, rm, k1inc1, pm, k to marker, rm, skp, *do not turn;* pm, k to end (you will be at the bottom of Diamond 1 in position to begin Diamond 3).

Step 3

Make Diamond 3.

Repeat the instructions for Diamond 2 until you have reached marker on the top of Diamond 1. Remove marker. Knit to the top corner of Diamond 2 (k1inc1 stitch), pm. Knit to the bottom of Diamond 2 to be in position for knitting Triangle 1.

Step 4

Make Triangle 1.

Row 1: K1inc1, skp, turn.

Row 2: S1, k2, turn.

Row 3: K1inc1, k1, skp, turn.

Row 4: S1, k3, turn.

Row 5: K1inc1, k2, skp, turn.

Row 6: S1, pm, k to end, turn.

Row 7: K1inc1, *yo, k1; rep from * to marker, rm, yo, skp, turn.

Row 8: Dropping all yo's, s1, pm, k to end, turn.

Rows 9 and 11: K1inc1, k to marker, rm, skp, turn.

Rows 10 and 12: S1, pm, k to end, turn.

Rep rows 7 to 12 until you have reached st before marker at top corner of Diamond 2. Work the following 2 rows:

Row 1: S1, k to end, turn.

Row 2: Bind off all sts along Triangle 1 edge, and continue binding off sts along Diamond 2 edge, and then continue binding off sts along Diamond 3 edge until you have reached top corner of Diamond 3. Knit to end (bottom of Diamond 3) to get into position for Triangle 2.

Step 5

Make Triangle 2.

Repeat the instructions for Triangle 1, except when you have reached the top corner of Diamond 3, bind off remaining sts of Triangle 2.

FINISHING

Cut yarn. Weave in ends.

THESE SHAWLS WERE KNIT WITH:

1 HANK BLUE HERON'S BEADED RAYON, 100% RAYON, 8OZ/227G = 525 YDS/480M, COLOR SANDSTONE

AND

4 SKEINS ARTYARN'S ROYAL SILK, 100% SILK, 1.8OZ/50G = 163 YDS/149M, COLOR #114 BURGUNDY

DIAMOND PANEL VEST

THIS VEST IS CONSTRUCTED BY KNITTING TWO DIAMOND MODULAR PANELS USING SHORT ROWS. THE PANELS ARE THEN CONNECTED TO MAKE THE VEST. AN INTERMEDIATE PROJECT, THIS IS A GOOD EXERCISE IN COMBINING DIFFERENT SHAPES AFTER YOU HAVE MADE SEVERAL SIMPLER PROJECTS.

MATERIALS

Approx total: 690yd/621m
(920yd/828m, 1050yd/945m)
worsted-weight wool yarn that knits
up at 20 sts to 4"/10cm

Knitting needles: 4.5mm (size 7 U.S.)
24"/61cm circular knitting needles *or
size to obtain gauge*

Crochet hook: 3.5mm (size E U.S.)

FINISHED MEASUREMENTS

Adult sizes: S (M, L)

Finished chest: 38¼"/98cm
(42"/107cm, 47¾"/121cm)

Finished length: 22"/56cm
(22¼"/56.5cm, 24"/61cm)

GAUGE

17 sts and 34 rows = 4"/10cm in
Garter Stitch

Always take time to check your gauge.

PATTERN STITCHES

DIAGONAL RIGHT AND SIDE
TRIANGLES
See page 28, and make a small practice swatch if you have never used
this technique before.

CENTER-INCREASE DIAMONDS
See page 51, and make a small practice swatch if you have never used
this technique before.

INSTRUCTIONS

Diamond Modular Panels (make 2)

Step 1

Make a Base Triangle.

Using the knitted cast on, CO 8 (9, 11) sts.

Row 1: K1tblinc1, k1, turn; pm, s1, k1, s1wyif, turn.

Row 2: K1tblinc1, k to marker, rm, k1, turn; pm, s1, k to last 1 st, s1wyif, turn.

Repeat row 2 until all 8 (9, 11) cast-on sts have been used up, ending with: k1tblinc1, k to marker, rm, k1— 15 (17, 21) sts, *do not turn*.

Step 2

Repeat instructions for Base Triangle to make a facing Base Triangle on other side.

Step 3

Make a Diamond.

Row 1: K1, turn.

Row 2: S1, k2, turn.

Row 3: S1, k1inc1, skp, turn.

Row 4: S1, k1inc1, pm, k1, skp, turn.

Row 5: S1, pm, k to marker, rm, k1inc1, pm, k1, skp, turn.

Row 6: S1, pm, k to marker, rm, k1inc1, pm, k to marker, rm, skp, turn.

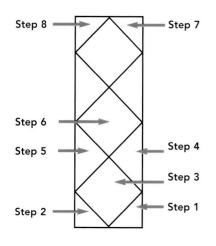

Step 8 → ← Step 7
Step 6 →
Step 5 → ← Step 4
← Step 3
Step 2 → ← Step 1

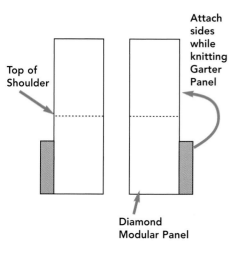

Top of Shoulder

Attach sides while knitting Garter Panel

Diamond Modular Panel

Repeat row 6 until all stitches of both Base Triangles have been used up—30 (34, 42) sts.

Step 4

Make a Side Triangle on one side of the diamond.

Row 1: K1tblinc1, skp, turn; s1, k1, s1wyif, turn.

Row 2: K1tblinc1, k1, skp, turn; s1, pm, k to last 1 st, s1wyif, turn.

Row 3: K1tblinc1, k to marker, rm, skp, turn; s1, pm, k to last 1 st, s1wyif, turn.

Repeat row 3 until Side Triangle has used up 14 (16, 20) sts of Diamond [14 (16, 20) sts in Side Triangle, 16 (18, 22) unknitted stitches left on Diamond] making sure on the last repeat of row 3 to end with: k1tblinc1, k12 (14, 18), rm, skp, *do not turn*.

Step 5

Knit 15 (17, 21) and work second facing Side Triangle on other side of Diamond by repeating Step 4.

Step 6

Repeat steps 3 to 5 ending with step 3 when you have completed 9 (8, 7) Diamonds.

Step 7

Make an End Triangle on one side of the Diamond—15 (17, 21) unknitted sts left on Diamond). K15 (17, 21) to bottom of other side of Diamond (to position for next End Triangle).

Row 1: K1tblinc1, skp, turn; s1, k1, s1wyif, turn.

Row 2: K1tblinc1, k1, skp, turn; s1, pm, k to last 1 st, s1wyif, turn.

Row 3: K1tblinc1, k to marker, rm, skp, turn; s1, pm, k to last 1 st, s1wyif, turn.

Repeat row 3 until you've used up 8 (9, 11) sts of Diamond—8 (9, 11) sts in End Triangle, and bind off top as follows:

Row 1: S1, k to marker, rm, skp, turn; s1, pm, k to last 1 st, s1, turn.

Row 2: S2psso, k to marker, rm, skp, turn; s1, pm, k to last 1 st, s1, turn.

Repeat row 2 until there are 3 sts left of End Triangle. S2psso, skp, bind off one time, k1, pass second stitch on right needle over stitch just knitted to bind off one stitch.

Step 8

Repeat instructions for End Triangle to make a facing End Triangle on other side of Diamond.

FINISHING

Cut yarn, weave in ends.

Vest Construction

Right Half of Vest: Fold down one Modular Diamond Panel in half—4 1/2 (4, 3 1/2) diamonds on each side. Both sides of Diamond Panel will be joined to form a single piece as in schematic above.

Row 1 (RS): Pick up and pull loop knit-wise through bottom most stitch of 1st half of Modular Diamond Panel's side, and using knitted cast on, CO an additional 28 (30, 32) sts. Pick up and pull loop purl-wise through bottommost stitch of second half of Modular Diamond Panel's side, making sure that Panel is not twisted—30 (32, 34) sts.

Row 2 (WS): K to last 1 st, s1, pick up 1 st by pulling loop knit-wise through stitch directly above stitch just slipped, psso—30 (32, 34) sts.

Row 3 (RS): S1, knit to last 1 st, s1, pick up 1 st by pulling loop purl-wise through stitch directly above stitch just slipped, psso—30 (32, 34) sts.

Row 4 (WS): S1, knit to last 1 st, s1, pick up 1 st by pulling loop knit-wise through stitch directly above stitch just slipped, psso—30 (32, 34) sts.

Repeat rows 3 and 4 a total of 41 (41, 45) times.

Left Half of Vest: Fold down one Modular Diamond Panel in half—4 1/2 (4, 3 1/2) diamonds on each side. Both sides of Diamond Panel will be joined to form a single piece as in schematic above.

Row 1 (RS): Pick up and pull loop purl-wise through bottommost stitch of 1st half of Modular Diamond Panel's side, and using the knitted cast on, CO an additional 28 (30, 32) sts. Pick up and pull loop knit-wise through bottommost stitch of second half of Modular Diamond Panel's side, making sure that Panel is not twisted—30 (32, 34) sts.

Row 2 (WS): K to last 1 st, s1, pick up 1 st by pulling loop purl-wise through stitch directly above stitch just slipped, psso—30 (32, 34) sts.

Row 3 (RS): S1, knit to last 1 st, s1, pick up 1 st by pulling loop knit-wise through stitch directly above stitch just slipped, psso—30 (32, 34) sts.

Row 4 (WS): S1, knit to last 1 st, s1, pick up 1 st by pulling loop purl-wise through stitch directly above stitch just slipped, psso—30 (32, 34) sts.

Repeat rows 3-4 a total of 41 (41, 45) times to match other half of vest.

Back: Connect the two halves you have just constructed by joining the exposed portions of the Modular

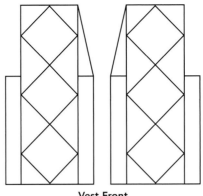

Vest Front

Diamond Panels together in the back as follows:

Row 1 (RS): Pick up and pull loop knit-wise through bottommost stitch of one of the Modular Diamond Panels, and using the knitted cast on, CO an additional 8 (11, 14) sts. Pick up and pull loop purl-wise through bottommost stitch of the other Modular Diamond Panel, making sure that the Panel is not twisted—10 (13, 16) sts.

Row 2 (WS): K to last 1 st, s1, pick up 1 st by pulling loop knit-wise through stitch directly above stitch just slipped, psso—10 (13, 16) sts.

Row 3 (RS): S1, knit to last 1 st, s1, pick up 1 st by pulling loop purl-wise through stitch directly above stitch just slipped, psso—10 (13, 16) sts.

Row 4 (WS): S1, knit to last 1 st, s1, pick up 1 st by pulling loop knit-wise through stitch directly above stitch just slipped, psso—10 (13, 16) sts.

Repeat rows 3 and 4 a total of 41 (41, 45) times.

Increase Row: S1, k to end, pick up 1 st by pulling loop purl-wise through stitch directly above last stitch just

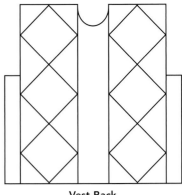

Vest Back

knitted, turn; s1, k to end, pick up 1 st by pulling loop knit-wise through stitch directly above stitch just knitted.

Repeat Increase Row a total of 1 time (12, 15, 18 sts), then rows 3 and 4 a total of 8 (9, 9) times, then Increase Row a total of 1 time (14, 17, 20 sts), then rows 3 and 4 a total of 8 (8, 9) times, then Increase Row 1 a total of 1 time (16, 19, 22 sts), then rows 3 and 4 a total of 8 (8, 8) times. Bind off all stitches, cut yarn.

Bands

Right Front Band: Holding right vest front facing you, pick up 1 stitch by pulling loop bottom most stitch in Diamond Modular Pattern. Using the knitted cast on, CO 7 sts.

Row 1 (RS): K7, s1, pick up 1 st by pulling loop purl-wise through stitch directly above stitch just slipped.

Row 2 (WS): S1, k6, p1.

Row 3 (RS): S1, k to last 1 st, s1, pick up 1 st by pulling loop purl-wise through stitch directly above stitch just slipped, psso.

Repeat rows 2 and 3 a total of 40 (40, 45) times.

Decrease Row: S1, k2tog, k to last 1 st, s1, pick up 1 st by pulling loop purl-wise through stitch directly above stitch just slipped, psso.

Continue as follows:

Decrease Row—7 sts.

Repeat rows 2 and 3 a total of 7 (7, 7) times.

Decrease Row—6 sts.

Repeat rows 2 and 3 a total of 3 (3, 3) times.

Decrease Row—5 sts.

Repeat rows 2 and 3 a total of 2 (3, 3) times.

Decrease Row—4 sts.

Repeat rows 2 and 3 a total of 2 (2, 3) times.

Decrease Row—3 sts.

Repeat rows 2 and 3 a total of 2 (2, 2) times.

Decrease Row—2 sts.

Repeat rows 2 and 3 a total of 2 (2, 2) times.

Decrease Row—1 st.

Repeat rows 2 and 3 a total of 2 (2, 2) times.

Left Front Band: Follow instructions for Right Front Band, but begin on WS, making sure to pull loop knit-wise throughout when picking up stitches along Diamond Modular Panel.

Armhole Edgings: With RS facing, attach yarn and sc with crochet hook into both loops of every edge stitch, ending with slip stitch. Cut yarn. Repeat on other sleeve.

Bottom and Front Edgings: Starting at one corner of vest with right side facing you, sc with crochet hook

into both loops of every edge stitch. Cut yarn.

Weave in all ends. Block lightly.

THIS VEST WAS KNIT WITH:

7 (9, 10) SKEINS OF ARTYARNS SUPERMERINO, 100% SUPERWASH MERINO WOOL, 1.8OZ/50G = 104 YD/95M PER SKEIN, COLOR #111, VARIEGATED BURGUNDY/RED

ELEGANT OPENWORK PONCHO

Today's ponchos are infinitely more stylish than the granny-square versions of the 1960s. With a flirty, curved front and a peek-a-boo lace stitch, this sheer rendition is elegant enough to wear to an evening party, or can jazz up your favorite turtleneck and jeans.

MATERIALS

Approx total: 690yd/621m (medium) to 1300yd/1170m (large) worsted-weight yarn that knits up at 20 sts to 4"/10cm

Knitting needles: 4mm (size 6 U.S.) *or size to obtain gauge*

4 stitch markers

1 stitch holder

FINISHED MEASUREMENTS

Small/Medium (Large/Extra-Large)

Side of the center-back Diamond measures approx 10"/25.4cm to 12"/30.5cm (small/medium) or 14"/35.6cm to 20"/50.8cm (large/extra-large)

GAUGE

17 stitches x 17 rows = 4 x 4" /10 x 10 cm square in Unmitered Squares pattern stitch with open-work rows

Always take time to check your gauge.

PATTERN STITCHES

DIAGONAL TRIANGLES
See page 28, and make a small practice swatch if you have never used this technique before.

CENTER-INCREASE SQUARES
See page 51, and make a small practice swatch if you have never used this technique before.

OPENWORK PARTITION
Work a yo between each knit stitch as indicated in pattern.

On the next row, drop the yarn overs to create elongated stitches.

INSTRUCTIONS

Note: The poncho is worked in one continuous piece, starting with Diamond 1, then Diamond 2, then Diamond 3, then a final Triangle. The two ends are joined with a three-needle bind-off.

Cast on 2 sts.

Step 1

Make Diamond 1.

Row 1: K1inc1, k1, turn—3 sts.

Row 2: K1inc1, k1inc1, k1, turn—5 sts.

Row 3: K1inc1, k1inc1, pm, k2, p1, turn—7 sts.

Rows 4 to 6: S1, k to marker, rm, k1inc1, pm, k to last 1 st, p1, turn.

Row 7: S1, ★yo, k1; rep from ★ to marker, rm, yo, k1inc1, pm ★yo, k1, rep to last 1 st, p1, turn.

Row 8: Dropping all yo's, s1, k to marker, rm, k1inc1, pm, k1, k to last 1 st, p1, turn.

Rows 9 to 12: S1, k to marker, rm, k1inc1, pm, k to last 1 st, p1, turn.

Repeat rows 7 to 12 until 1 side of diamond measures 10 to 12"/25.4 to 30.4cm (small/medium) or 14 to 20"/35.5 to 50.8cm (large/extra-large).

Note: This Diamond should cover your entire back and should extend from the neck down as far as you'd like shawl to reach. To make the shawl larger, continue repeating rows 7 to 12 until the diamond is the desired size.

Last row: S1, k to marker, rm, k1inc1, pm, k to end, turn.

Step 2

Make Diamond 2.

Following the order in the diagram below, end at one of the corners of Diamond 1 and begin Diamond 2 as follows:

Row 1: K1inc1, turn; s1, k1, turn— 2 sts.

Row 2: K1inc1, skp, turn; s1, k1inc1, p1, turn—4 sts.

Row 3: S1, k1inc1, k1, skp, turn— 5 sts.

Row 4: S1, pm, k1, k1inc1, pm, k1, p1, turn.

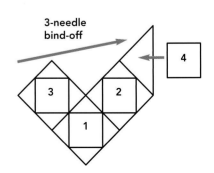

3-needle bind-off

Row 5: S1, k to marker, rm, k1inc1, pm, k to marker, rm, skp. turn.

Row 6: S1, pm, k to marker, rm, k1inc1, pm, k to last 1 st, p1, turn.

Row 7: S1, *yo, k1; rep from * to marker, rm, yo, k1inc1, pm *yo, k1, rep to marker, rm, yo, skp.

Row 8: Dropping all yo's, s1, pm, k to marker, rm, k1inc1, pm, k to last 1 st, p1.

Rows 9 and 11: S1, k to marker, rm, k1inc1, pm, k to marker, rm, skp, turn.

Rows 10 and 12: S1, pm, k to marker, rm, k1inc1, pm, k to last 1 st, p1.

Rep rows 7 to 12 until you have reached marker on previously knitted Diamond 1. Remove marker. Knit the last 2 rows of Diamond 2 as follows:

Row 1: S1, pm, k to marker, rm, k1inc1, pm, k to last 1 st, p1.

Row 2: S1, k to marker, rm, k1inc1, k to marker, rm, skp, *do not turn;* pm, k to end (you will be at the bottom of Diamond 1 in position to begin Diamond 3).

Step 3

Make Diamond 3.

Repeat the instructions above (as for Diamond 2) until you have reached the marker on the top of Diamond 1. Remove marker. Knit to top corner of Diamond 2 (K1inc1 stitch), pm. Knit to bottom of Diamond 2 and turn to be in position for knitting Triangle 1.

Step 4

Make Triangle.

Row 1: K1inc1, skp, turn.

Row 2: S1, k2, turn.

Row 3: K1inc1, k1, skp, turn.

Row 4: S1, k3, turn.

Row 5: K1inc1, k2, skp, turn.

Row 6: S1, pm, k to end, turn.

Row 7: K1inc1, *yo, k1; rep from * to marker, rm, yo, skp, turn.

Row 8: Dropping all yo's, s1, pm, k to end, turn.

Rows 9 and 11: K1inc1, k to marker, rm, skp, turn.

Rows 10 and 12: S1, pm, k to end, turn.

Rep rows 7 to 12 until you have reached st before marker at top corner of Diamond 2. Work the following 2 rows:

Row 1: S1, k to end, turn.

Row 2: Place all sts along Triangle 1 edge on stitch holder, continue binding off sts along Diamond 2 edge, and then continue binding off sts along Diamond 3 edge until you have reached top corner of Diamond 3.

Move all stitches from stitch holder onto 2nd needle. Using the three-needle bind-off (see page 17 for instructions), bind off all stitches from the Triangle 1 edge and the Diamond 3 edge together.

FINISHING

Cut yarn, weave in ends.

THIS PONCHO WAS KNIT WITH:

5 SKEINS OF ARTYARNS ULTRAMERINO 6, 100% MERINO WOOL, 1.8OZ/50G = 138YD/126M, COLOR #104

COZY DIAMOND WRAP

HIS SHAWL, WITH MULTIPLE SHAPES AND COLORS, PROVIDES A FUN CHALLENGE FOR EXPERIENCED KNITTERS. MADE FROM WORSTED-WEIGHT WOOL, IT IS WARM ENOUGH TO WEAR EVEN DURING THE COLDEST MONTHS OF WINTER. PAMPER YOURSELF WITH TWO: ONE TO WEAR ON EVENINGS OUT, AND ONE TO WRAP AROUND YOUR SHOULDERS ON CHILLY NIGHTS WHILE READING IN BED.

INSTRUCTIONS

Step 1

Make Right Side Half Triangle (in A).

With A, and using the knitted cast on, CO 4 sts.

Row 1: K1inc1, turn; s1, k1, turn.

Row 2: K1inc1, k2; turn, s1, k3, turn.

Row 3: K1inc1, k4, turn; s1, k5, turn.

Row 4: K1inc1, k6—8 sts.

Step 2

Make Bottom Equilateral Triangle Panel (in A).

Using the knitted cast on, CO 8 sts.

Row 1: K8 (knitting back along same sts just cast on), turn (you will now continue to work the same 8 sts).

Row 2: K1inc1, turn; s1—1 st (of equilateral triangle) left unknitted, turn.

Row 3: K1inc1, k1, turn; s1, k1—2 sts left unknitted, turn.

Row 4: K1inc1, k2, turn; s1, k2—3 sts left unknitted, turn.

Row 5: K1inc1, k3, turn; s1, k3—4 sts left unknitted, turn.

Row 6: K1inc1, k4, turn; s1, k4—5 sts left unknitted, turn.

Row 7: K1inc1, k5, turn; s1, k5—6 sts left unknitted, turn.

Row 8: K1inc1, k6, turn; s1, k6—7 sts left unknitted, turn.

Row 9: K1inc1, k7, turn; s1, k7—8 sts left unknitted, turn.

Row 10: K1inc1, k7.

Repeat Step 2 twelve more times across row—13 equilateral triangles.

MATERIALS

Approx total: 600yd/548m worsted-weight yarn that knits up at 20 sts to 4"/10cm

Color A: 300yd/274m in olive

Color B: 300yd/274m in gold

40 yd/37m fur yarn for trim

Knitting needles: 4.5 mm (size 7 U.S.) 29"/74cm circular needles *or size to obtain gauge*

Crochet hook: 5mm (size H U.S.)

3 stitch markers

FINISHED MEASUREMENTS

50"/127cm long x 18"/45.7cm wide including fur trim

GAUGE

8 stitch x 8 stitch Diamond = 2" width x 2" length/5 x 5cm

Always take time to check your gauge.

PATTERN STITCHES

DIAGONAL UPRIGHT EQUILATERAL TRIANGLES AND SQUARES
See page 28, and make a small practice swatch if you have never used this technique before.

CENTER-INCREASE DIAMONDS
See page 51, and make a small practice swatch if you have never used this technique before.

Step 3

Make Left Half Triangle (in A).

Using the knitted cast on, CO 4 sts.

Work rows 1 to 3 of Step 1.

Row 4: K1inc1, k6, turn; s1, k7—8 sts. Turn and drop A, do not cut.

Slip 8 sts onto right needle. Attach B.

Step 4

Make Center-Increase Diamond Panel (in B).

Row 1: With B, k2, turn.

Row 2: S1, k1inc1, skp, turn.

Row 3: S1, k1inc1, pm1, k1, skp, turn.

Row 4: S1, pm2, k to marker1, rm1, k1inc1, pm1, k1, skp, turn.

Row 5: S1, pm3, k to marker1, rm1, k1inc1, pm1, k to marker2, rm2, skp, turn.

Row 6: S1, pm2, k to marker 1, rm1, k1inc1, pm1, k to marker3, rm3, skp, turn.

Repeat rows 5 and 6 four more times.

Last row: S1, k6, rm1, k1inc1, k7, rm2, skp, *do not turn*—17 sts (on diamond).

K7, *do not turn*.

Repeat Step 4 until there are 13 Center-Increase Diamonds across panel. Work 14th Center-Increase Diamond as follows:

Repeat rows 5 and 6 four more times, removing all markers on the last row.

Last row: S1, k7, drop B, *do not turn*. Slip back 8 sts onto the right needle so all sts are on the same side. Slide work to other end of circular needle and pick up A.

Step 5

Make Left Side Diagonal Triangle (in A).

Row 1: With A, k1inc1, skp, turn; s1, pm, k to end.

Row 2: K1inc1, knit to marker, rm, skp, turn; s1, pm, k to end.

Repeat row 2 until there are 7 sts on the right needle.

Last row: K1inc1, k to marker, rm, skp—8 sts on the right needle.

Step 6

Make Diagonal Diamonds Panel (in A).

Row 1: K1inc1, k6, skp, turn.

Row 2: S1, k7, turn.

Repeat rows 1 and 2 a total of 7 times. K1inc1, k6, skp, *do not turn*. Make a total of 13 diagonal diamonds. After the last diamond is complete, k9.

Step 7

Make a Right Side Diagonal Triangle (in A).

Repeat Step 5.

Last Row: S1, k to end (diagonal diamond panel complete). Drop A. Slide 8 sts onto the right needle. Pick up B.

Repeat Steps 4 to 7, ending with Step 4 when Shawl measures 18"/45.7cm or desired width.

Step 8

Make Ending Triangle Panel (in A).

Bind the shapes off as follows:

First Half Triangle

Row 1: With A, k1inc1, skp, turn; s1, k2, turn.

Row 2: K1inc1, k1, skp, turn; s1, k3, turn.

Row 3: K1inc1, k2, skp, turn; s1, k3, s1wyif, turn.

Row 4: S2psso, k2, skp, turn; s1, k2, s1wyif, turn.

Row 5: S2psso, k1, skp, turn; s1, k1, s1wyif, turn.

Row 6: S2psso, skp, pass 2nd st on right needle over 1st —1 st on rh needle, *do not turn.*

13 End Triangles

Row 1: BO 1 st, k6, skp, turn; s1, k6, s1wyif, turn.

Row 2: S2psso, k5, skp, turn; s1, k5, s1wyif, turn.

Row 3: S2psso, k4, skp, turn; s1, k4, s1wyif, turn.

Row 4: S2psso, k3, skp, turn; s1, k3, s1wyif, turn.

Row 5: S2psso, k2, skp, turn; s1, k2, s1wyif, turn.

Row 6: S2psso, k1, skp, turn; s1, k1, s1wyif, turn.

Row 7: S2psso, skp, pass 2nd st on right needle over 1st—1 st rem on right needle. Bind off 1 st, *do not turn.*

Repeat rows 1 to 7 of End Triangles twelve more times.

When 13 End Triangles have been completed, BO 2 sts, k8.

Last Half Triangle

Repeat rows 1 to 6 of First Half Triangle. Bind off last st.

FINISHING

Cut yarn, weave in ends.

Fur Trim

Using crochet hook and fur, single crochet into every stitch on narrow end of the shawl. ★Turn; chain 2. Work double crochet across row. Repeat from ★ 3 times or until desired fluffiness is attained. Repeat on opposite end of the shawl.

THIS SHAWL WAS KNIT WITH:

6 SKEINS OF ARTYARNS SUPERMERINO, 100% MERINO WOOL, 1.8OZ/50G = 104YD/95M:

(A) 3 SKEINS COLOR #119 OLIVE

(B) 3 SKEINS COLOR #102 GOLD

1 SKEIN OF ARTYARNS SILK FUR, 90% SILK/10% NYLON, 0.9OZ/25G = 48YD/44M, COLOR #119 OLIVE

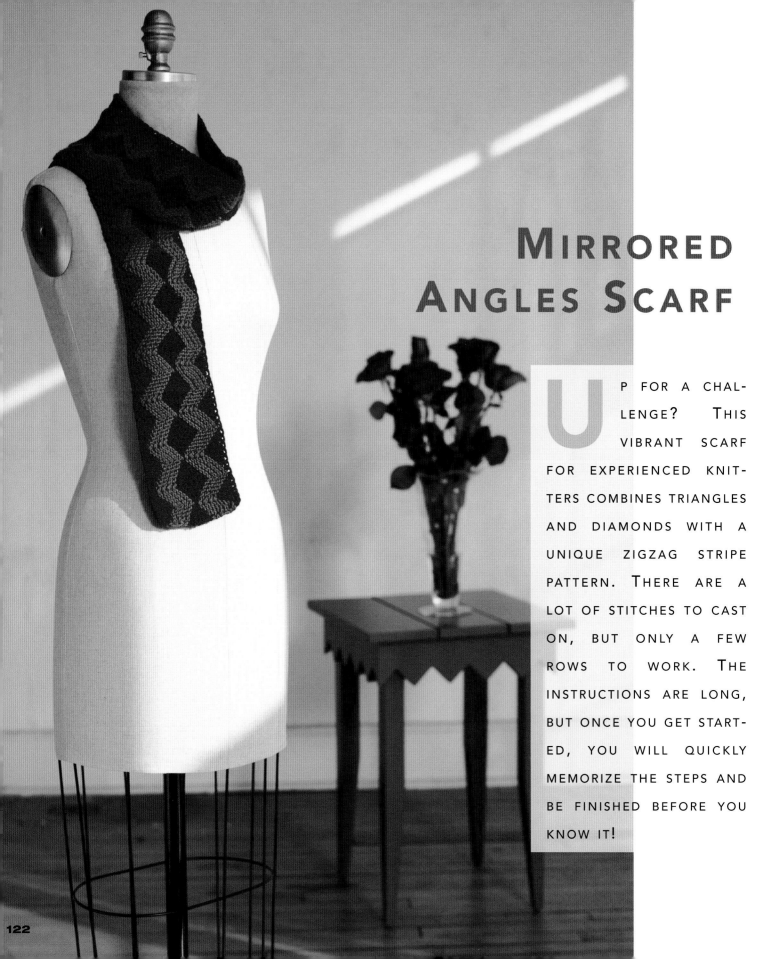

MIRRORED ANGLES SCARF

UP FOR A CHAL-LENGE? THIS VIBRANT SCARF FOR EXPERIENCED KNIT-TERS COMBINES TRIANGLES AND DIAMONDS WITH A UNIQUE ZIGZAG STRIPE PATTERN. THERE ARE A LOT OF STITCHES TO CAST ON, BUT ONLY A FEW ROWS TO WORK. THE INSTRUCTIONS ARE LONG, BUT ONCE YOU GET START-ED, YOU WILL QUICKLY MEMORIZE THE STEPS AND BE FINISHED BEFORE YOU KNOW IT!

INSTRUCTIONS

Note: This scarf is worked sideways, so that the length of the scarf is determined upon cast on. If you would like to lengthen or shorten the scarf, do so in multiples of 7 sts. You may prefer to use the knitted cast-on method, whereby with A, cast on 7 sts, knit back across the 7 sts, complete 1 triangle, then use the knitted cast on to cast on another 7 stitches, knit back across the 7 sts, complete the 2nd triangle, and so on. This will allow you to more accurately predetermine the length of your scarf.

With A, loosely cast on 182 sts to start with 26 triangles of 7 stitches each.

Step 1

Make Base Triangles.

Triangle 1:

Row 1: K1inc1, turn.

Row 2: S1, turn.

Row 3: K1inc1, k1, turn.

Row 4: S1, k1, turn.

Row 5: K1inc1, k2, turn.

Row 6: S1, k2, turn.

Row 7: K1inc1, k3, turn.

Row 8: S1, k3, turn.

Row 9: K1inc1, k4, turn.

Row 10: S1, k4, turn.

Row 11: K1inc1, k5, turn.

Row 12: S1, k5, turn.

Row 13: K1inc1, k6, *do not turn.*

Triangles 2 to 26:

Repeat rows 1 to 13 of Triangle 1.

Cut A. Slide work so that you are starting with stitches from Triangle 1. Attach B.

Step 2

Make Zigzag Panel.

Note: The k1inc1 of the first row of zigzag stripes should be in the same

MATERIALS

Approx total: 240yd/219m light worsted yarn that knits up at 21 sts to 4"/10cm

Color A: 60yd/55m in red

Color B: 60yd/55m in orange

Color C: 60yd/55m in pink

Color D: 60yd/55m in purple

Knitting needles: 5mm (size 8 U.S.) circular needle at least 29"/74cm long *or size to obtain gauge*

FINISHED MEASUREMENTS

52"/132.1cm long x 5"/12.7cm wide

GAUGE

7 st and 12 row Base Triangle (step 1) = 2"/5cm wide

Always take time to check your gauge.

PATTERN STITCHES

DIAGONAL UPRIGHT TRIANGLES
See page 28, and make a small practice swatch if you have never used these techniques before.

BULL'S-EYE SQUARES
See page 68, and make a small practice swatch if you have never used these techniques before.

ZIGZAG PANEL
Knit across the entire row increasing at the top of each triangle and decreasing at the bottom as indicated in the pattern.

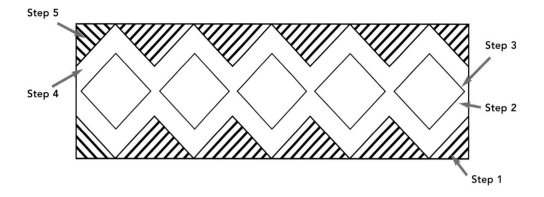

place on top of each of the base tri-angles, and the k2tog should be in the same place between the two triangles.

Row 1: With B, s1,★k5, k1inc1, k6, k2tog; rep from ★ to last triangle. K5, k1inc1, k6, s1, turn.

Row 2: With B, skp, ★k5, k1inc1, k6, k2tog; rep from ★ to last triangle. K5, k1inc1, k6, s1, turn.

Rows 3 and 4: Repeat row 2. Cut B. Attach C.

Rows 5 to 8: Repeat row 2 with C. Cut C. Attach D.

Step 3

Make Bull's-Eye Diamonds.

1st Half-Diamond for Scarf Bottom:

Row 1: With D, skp, k6, turn.

Row 2: S1, k4, k2tog, turn.

Row 3: S1, k4, turn.

Row 4: S1, k2, k2tog, turn.

Row 5: S1, k2, turn.

Row 6: S1, k2tog, turn.

Row 7: K1inc1, k1, turn.

Row 8: S1, k2, turn.

Row 9: K1inc1, k3, turn.

Row 10: S1, k4, turn.

Row 11: K1inc1, k5, *do not turn.*

Diamonds 2 to 24:

Row 1: K6, k2tog, k6, turn.

Row 2: S1, k5, k2tog, k5, turn.

Row 3: S1, k4, k2tog, k4, turn.

Row 4: S1, k3, k2tog, k3, turn.

Row 5: S1, k2, k2tog, k2, turn.

Row 6: S1, k1, k2tog, k1, turn.

Row 7: S1, k2tog, turn.

Row 8: K1inc1, turn.

Row 9: K1inc1, k1, m1k1, turn.

Row 10: S1, k1, k1inc1, k1, m1k1, turn.

Row 11: S1, k1, k1inc1, k3, m1k1, turn.

Row 12: S1, k3, k1inc1, k3, m1k1, turn.

Row 13: S1, k3, k1inc1, k5, m1k1, turn.

Row 14: S1, k5, k1inc1, k5, m1k1, turn.

Row 15: S1, k5, k1inc1, k6, k2tog, k5, k2tog, k6, turn.

Repeat rows 2 to 15 for Diamonds 2 to 24.

Diamond 25:

Repeat rows 2 to 14 of Diamonds 2-24.

End with: S1, k5, k1inc1, k7, *do not turn.*

Last Half-Diamond:

Row 1: K5, k2tog, turn.

Row 2: S1, k5, turn.

Row 3: S1, k3, k2tog.

Row 4: S1, k3, turn.

Row 5: S1, k1, k2tog, turn.

Row 6: S1, k1, turn.

Row 7: K2tog, turn.

Row 8: K1inc1, k1, turn.

Row 9: S1, k2, turn.

Row 10: K1inc1, k3, turn.

Row 11: S1, k4, turn.

Row 12: K1inc1, k5, turn.

Row 13: S1, k6.

Cut D. Slide work so that you are starting with stitches from Triangle 1. Attach C.

Step 4

Make Reverse Zigzag Panel.

Row 1: With C, k6, *k2tog, k5, k1inc1, k6; repeat from * to last 8 sts. K2tog, k6.

Row 2: K6, k2tog, k5, *k1inc1, k6, k2tog, k5; repeat from * to end.

Row 3: K1inc1, k4, k2tog, k5, *k1inc1, k6, k2tog, k5; repeat from * to last 5 sts. K5.

Row 4: Repeat row 3. Cut C, attach B.

Rows 5 to 8: With B, k1inc1, k4, k2tog, k5, *k1inc1, k6, k2tog, k5; repeat from * to end.

Cut B, attach A.

Step 5

Make Ending Triangles.

Row 1: With A, k1inc1, k4, skp, turn.

Row 2: S1, k6, turn.

Row 3: K1inc1, k5, skp, turn.

Row 4: S1, k6, s1, turn.

Row 5: Skp, k5, skp, turn.

Row 6: S1, k5, s1, turn.

Row 7: Skp, k4, skp, turn.

Row 8: S1, k4, s1, turn.

Row 9: Skp, k3, skp, turn.

Row 10: S1, k3, s1, turn.

Row 11: Skp, k2, skp, turn.

Row 12: S1, k2, s1, turn.

Row 13: Skp, bind off next 3 stitches, k6, skp, turn.

Row 14: S1, k6, s1, turn.

Row 15: Skp, k5, skp, turn.

Row 16: S1, k5, s1, turn.

Row 17: Skp, k4, skp, turn.

Row 18: S1, k4, s1, turn.

Row 19: Skp, k3, skp, turn.

Row 20: S1, k3, s1, turn.

Row 21: Skp, k2, skp, turn.

Row 22: S1, k2, s1, turn.

Row 23: Skp, k1, skp, turn.

Row 24: S1, k1, s1, turn.

Row 25: Skp, bind off next 2 sts, k6, skp, turn.

Repeat rows 14 to 25 across row to last triangle, then repeat rows 14 to 22, skp, and bind off remaining sts.

FINISHING

Cut yarn, weave in ends.

THIS SCARF WAS KNIT WITH:

KARABELLA YARNS' AURORA 8, 100% MERI-NO WOOL, 1.8OZ/50G = APPROX 98YD/90M:

(A) 1 BALL COLOR #7 FIRE

(B) 1 BALL COLOR #8 ORANGE

(C) 1 BALL COLOR #24 PINK

(D) 1 BALL COLOR #21 FUCHSIA

ACKNOWLEDGMENTS

This book would not have been possible were it not for the support and encouragement of so many people.

First I'd like to thank Donna Druchunas, herself an author of the incredible book, *The Knitted Rug* (Lark 2004), who edited my book and literally whipped it into shape with her immediate grasp of what was required. This was no easy venture, and I was so thankful to have her help.

I'd also like to thank everyone at Lark who had a hand in producing this book. Deborah Morgenthal and Rebecca Guthrie helped all along the way with so many things that I can't list them here. Dana Irwin and Lance Wille turned my manuscript from simple text files into this gorgeous book. Orrin Lundgren created all of the illustrations. Many thanks also to cover designer, Barbara Zaretsky, and photographer John Widman.

My mother, Ruth, was incredible throughout the process. She not only taught me to knit at a young age, but helped knit many of the samples that are photographed here. Any time there was a crisis she dropped everything she was doing to knit for me. Her assistance, along with that of my sister Rita, was crucial in meeting my deadlines.

Thanks also to Jim and Terry for providing the beautiful rosewood and ebony needles that their company, Colonial Needles, manufactures. Knitting with those needles is like driving an incredibly luxurious car! It's hard to go back. A special thank you to Fanny, who proved that age is not a barrier to learning new knitting skills.

Jo, Jan, and Peg, you gave wonderful suggestions for improving the patterns, and the book is greatly improved thanks to you. Barbara the listmom, thank you for being patient with me while I've been too busy to post, and I greatly appreciate that you put me in touch with so many wonderful people, including Gloria and Karen. The many emails I've received from the modular tutorial subscribers have been incredibly motivating and I thank all of you. Gloria J., you encouraged me in more ways than you can imagine, particularly when you researched the history of modular knitting both in the U.S. and abroad and determined that my particular methods had not been used before. Thank you for all the materials that you sent me and the help you offered. Ditte, you had all my modular patterns translated and published in Danish—thank you for your faith in my designs and your encouragement. Pam and Lee, I'll always remember that you believed in my patterns from the beginning. Judi, your friendship means so much to me, and your help along the way has been terrific.

Diane and Janice of INKnitters, you helped pull together two patterns that were used in this book, and I thank you for your assistance. Diane, you actually came up with the idea of the Diamond Paneled Vest.

Cynthia, it has been wonderful having your assistance in yet another book—that makes two of them. Your feedback, encouragement, and enthusiasm are unsurpassed. Cynthia, Vanessa, Phyllis, and Laurie, thanks for setting up modular knitting workshops in your lovely shops. The students who attended have unknowingly contributed to this book in many, many ways. I learned so much from you, thank you.

To all the yarn companies who provided yarn for this project, thank you so much. And a big thank you to everyone whom I have inadvertently omitted but owe gratitude.

And last but not least, the three men in my life who do not knit but put up with how knitting has taken over more than one room in our house—Elliot, Jason, and Owen, you are the greatest!

ABOUT THE AUTHOR

ris Schreier is the author of *Reversible Knits* (Lark Books, 2009), *Lacy Little Knits* (Lark Books, 2007), and is the co-author of *Exquisite Little Knits* (Lark Books, 2004). Her original and innovative techniques are being used in knitting workshops and design schools around the world, and her patterns have been translated into multiple languages. Iris has appeared on various television shows and has written articles and published patterns for leading knitting magazines. She founded Artyarns to produce yarns and color combinations for her designs that were not available commercially. The company's world-renowned line of yarns now encompasses unusual and intriguing combinations of fibers— some with embellishments—that are all hand-painted in luscious colorways to work optimally with her patterns. To view more of Iris's designs and yarns and watch videos of her techniques, visit www.irisknits.com. Iris lives and works in White Plains, New York.

INDEX

Backwards knitting 16

Bull's-eye square 68–69, 72–75

Center-decrease shapes 80–95

Closing holes 15

Cut-out knitting 68–71, 76–79

Designing projects 18

Diamonds 30

Equilateral upright triangles 30

Experience levels 11, 12

Felting 41

Garter stitch squares, vertical and horizontal 19–25

Gauge 11

Knitted cast on 15

Knitting abbreviations 13

Loose bind-off 16

Loose cast on 14–15

Making I-cord 17, 79

Mitered square 82–83

Mitered triangle 82–83

Modules, growing 14

Multiple shapes, working with 96–125

Needles 12

Picking up stitches 17

Right diagonal triangles 30

Short rows 14

Side equilateral triangles 30

Stitch count 11

Stitch markers 14, 51

Techniques 14–17

Three-needle bind-off 17

Triangles and diamonds, diagonal 26–47

Unmitered shapes (center-increase shapes) 48–65

Yarn 12